CULTIVATED PALATE

The Arboretum Foundation

The mission of The Arboretum Foundation is to ensure stewardship for the Washington Park Arboretum, a Pacific Northwest treasure, and to provide horticultural leadership for the region. This stewardship requires effective leadership, stable funding, and broad public support.

on recycled paper

Printed in the USA by

WIMMER
The Wimmer Companies, Inc.
Memphis • Dallas

Front: Cover *Berberis nervosa*
Back Cover: Legume collection, with *Gleditsia triacanthos, Genista* spp., and *Cytisus* spp.

Azalea Way

CULTIVATED PALATE

The Arboretum Foundation Cookbook
c/o University of Washington, XD-10
Seattle, WA 98195
Phone: (206) 325-4510 FAX: (206) 325-8893

ॐ

Ordered by:

Name _____

Address _____

City _____ State _____ Zip _____

[ ] Check or money order enclosed. Please make checks payable
to The Arboretum Foundation.

*If gift, enclosure card to read: _____

Ship to: (If sent to another address)*

Name _____

Address _____

City _____ State _____ Zip _____

Please charge to my   ☐ Mastercard   ☐ Visa

Card # _____

Expiration Date _____

Signature of Cardholder _____

Proceeds from the sale of this book will enhance the Washington Park Arboretum

Please send _____ copies: @ 21.95 each

Add postage and handling: @ 3.00 each

Washington State Residents add sales tax @ 1.80 each

Total $ _____

CULTIVATED PALATE

The Arboretum Foundation Cookbook
c/o University of Washington, XD-10
Seattle, WA 98195
Phone: (206) 325-4510 FAX: (206) 325-8893

ॐ

Ordered by:

Name _____

Address _____

City _____ State _____ Zip _____

[ ] Check or money order enclosed. Please make checks payable
to The Arboretum Foundation.

*If gift, enclosure card to read: _____

Ship to: (If sent to another address)*

Name _____

Address _____

City _____ State _____ Zip _____

Please charge to my   ☐ Mastercard   ☐ Visa

Card # _____

Expiration Date _____

Signature of Cardholder _____

Proceeds from the sale of this book will enhance the Washington Park Arboretum

Please send _____ copies: @ 21.95 each

Add postage and handling: @ 3.00 each

Washington State Residents add sales tax @ 1.80 each

Total $ _____

TABLE OF CONTENTS

Rhododendron occidentale

DEDICATION

The recipes in this book, contributed by members of The Arboretum Foundation, garden lovers all, reflect their interest in and appreciation of good food. Whether they garden large plots or small, in containers or window boxes, or only browse the glories of Washington Park Arboretum, they are in tune with the environment and the natural splendors of the Pacific Northwest. Their recipes are not only delicious and healthy, but they also take into consideration the management of that rarest of commodities, time. You will sense an awareness of the seasonal and regional bounty available in garden, market, woods and sea. The recipes utilize fresh local ingredients in imaginative and innovative ways.

These home-tested recipes come from people who give countless volunteer hours to The Arboretum Foundation with energy, enthusiasm and fellowship in support of the Washington Park Arboretum.

The Unit Council is proud to dedicate this book to our generous volunteers, who enjoy learning from and giving to the Arboretum. They carry on a long and rich tradition, cherishing the close friendships that develop in the mutual nurturing of their favorite garden.

Japanese Garden, stone bridge and lantern

THE ARBORETUM FOUNDATION STORY

A diverse and important collection of trees and shrubs from all over the world grow in the heart of Seattle on the 200 gently rolling acres of Washington Park Arboretum.

It all began in the late 1930's when a small group of garden enthusiasts and civic activists saw in the narrow valley of undeveloped land between Madison Street and Lake Washington a possible location for an Arboretum. Their vision became a reality when the land was laid out by the famous Olmstead Brothers landscape firm of Boston.

Not long after the inception of the Washington Park Arboretum, The Arboretum Foundation was formed to further the project and to allow a maximum of citizen participation. The University of Washington's Center for Urban Horticulture is responsible for the plant collections, for their display and conservation, as well as for their use for education and research. The City of Seattle owns the land and provides for its maintenance through the Parks and Recreation Department. The Arboretum Foundation, a non-profit, open-membership organization with more than 3,000 members, constitutes an enthusiastic and dedicated support group for this beautiful place.

Besides making outright gifts to the Washington Park Arboretum, most notably the Graham Visitors Center, the Japanese Garden and the Tea House, The Foundation provides funds to augment staff salaries, for extra ground maintenance crews and for other necessities not covered by University and City budgets.

Immediately following the formation of The Arboretum Foundation, co-founder Juanita Graham organized working groups called Units. Their purpose was not only to support the Arboretum when and wherever needed, but also to provide opportunities for members to learn gardening and horticulture. Today members in 54 Units are an active and dynamic component of The Arboretum Foundation membership. Their role continues to expand as the perceived potential of Washington Park Arboretum grows, new gardens and collections are added, old ones renovated, and new services and programs are contemplated.

The Unit Council, a coordination group made up of representatives from every Unit, makes it possible for the Units to act together, especially in matters of fund raising.

The earliest fund raisers were Garden Tours and a Spring Plant Sale. Now, 50 years later, it takes 500 volunteers working all year to prepare and run the Spring Plant Sale which annually nets in excess of $25,000.

Liriodendron tulipifera

The Foundation's Spring Plant Sale has long been noted for the rare and unusual plants offered.

Some of the plants still come from members' gardens while others are grown from cuttings taken from plants in the Arboretum. The bulk of the plant material is brought in by specialist growers who donate a generous percentage of their sales to The Arboretum Foundation.

In 1959 The Arboretum Foundation funded the building of the Patricia Calvert Greenhouse in order to give members an opportunity to learn plant propagation and to increase the availability of rare and unusual plant material from Arboretum stock. It is staffed by volunteers, learning as they work, and is open to all members. Rooted cuttings and seedlings from the greenhouse are for sale in the Graham Visitors Center.

As the Arboretum matured and as more and more people began to appreciate its beauty, requests for guided walks led to the establishment of a training program for volunteer guides. The first tours highlighted native Northwest plants. Today trained tour guides lead groups through all of the specialized collections and gardens on a regular schedule.

As increasing numbers of primary and middle schools requested that students be given the experience of nature walks in the Arboretum, the Saplings Program was born. Every year several thousand children participate in the program, learning to recognize our native trees and shrubs and to understand the importance of environmental stewardship.

The Unit Council makes a conscious effort to involve gardeners throughout the Puget Sound region through public lectures, workshops and demonstrations usually held at the Graham Visitors Center. Newly formed Units receive help in program guidance and are made aware through the published monthly Newsletter and the Arboretum Bulletin of the many opportunities to volunteer and learn.

Study groups which concentrate on a particular plant genus or aspect of gardening meet regularly at the Graham Visitors Center both in the evening and during the day. They are open to all members free of charge.

Garden tours organized by members occur in the spring, summer and fall. Some are local, others go far afield; recently a group visited gardens in Ireland.

More than half of The Arboretum Foundation members belong to Units. Through the leadership of The Unit Council they have established four major annual fund-raising

Amelanchier spp. below Lookout

projects: the Spring Plant Sale, the October Bulb Sale, Greens Galore in late November, which offers an assortment of Christmas greens and decorating ideas, and the Used Book Sale in March. In addition many of the Units hold individual fund raisers.

The Northwest Flower and Garden Show in February has presented The Arboretum Foundation with a further opportunity to raise funds for the Arboretum. The Foundation sponsors the show's elegant Preview Party and also design and set up a full scale garden in the show. Two booths in the commercial section of the show present the wares of our Gift and Book Shop.

We proudly salute the more than 3000 members of The Arboretum Foundation and The Unit Council. They are magnificently fulfilling their wide-ranging mission to beautify and enhance Seattle's great treasure, the Washington Park Arboretum.

Callicarpa bodinieri

COOKBOOK CO-CHAIRS

꙾

Barbara Keightley   Mary Ellen Mulder

THE COMMITTEE

꙾

Janie Anderson	Harriett Litt
Debbie Andrews	Anne Martin
Vernette Cunningham	Kay Mayhew
Barby Doss	Elizabeth Moses
Lynn Garvey	Nancy Davidson Short
Betty Gray	Carol Simons
Gerry Holley	Joy Spurr
Karole Kiefer	Janet Patrick
Tina Kuhnle	Mary Thorne
Frances Kwapil	Joanne White
Rita Lambro	Molly Wolfe

SPECIAL ADVISORS

꙾

Christine Evans   Karen Krager

BENEFACTORS

꙾

Barbara and Jacob Engelstein

Japanese Garden, harbor with *Wisteria*
Overleaf: Winter Garden with *Hamamelis* and *Erica* x *darleyensis*

STARTERS

Blue Cheese Wheel with Basil and Walnuts   *Makes 3 Cups*

1   *cup fresh basil leaves*
½   *cup walnuts*
8   *ounces blue cheese, divided*
8   *ounces cream cheese, divided*
3   *tablespoons dry sherry*
    assorted crackers

- Finely chop basil leaves and walnuts in food processor. Add 2 tablespoons of blue cheese and 1 tablespoon of cream cheese; blend until smooth. Remove mixture from food processor; set aside.
- Put remaining blue cheese, cream cheese and sherry into food processor; blend until smooth.
- Line a 3-cup glass bowl with plastic wrap. Layer half of cheese mixture in bowl; add basil mixture, smoothing out layers. Top with second half of cheese mixture; cover with plastic wrap. Chill.
- About ½ hour before serving, unmold onto a serving platter. Surround with crackers and serve.

Many appetizers make a great lunch!

HOT MUSHROOM TARTS

Makes 27 Tarts

1   *3-ounce package cream cheese*
½   *cup butter*
1   *cup flour*
½   *pound fresh mushrooms, cleaned and trimmed*
¼   *cup fresh parsley*
5   *green onions, including 2 to 3 inches of green stem*
3   *tablespoons butter*
2   *tablespoons vegetable oil*
½   *teaspoon salt*
¾   *teaspoon ground marjoram*
6   *tablespoons grated Parmesan cheese*
6   *tablespoons fine bread crumbs*

- Cream together the cream cheese and butter. Add flour and mix well. Make about 27 balls from the dough and place in small tartlet or muffin pans. Press dough into bottoms and up sides of pans. Chill 1 hour.
- In a food processor, finely chop mushrooms. Add parsley and green onions, processing only until minced.
- In a medium frying pan, heat butter and oil. Add mushrooms, onions and parsley. Sauté over medium heat for about 6 minutes. Remove from heat and add salt, marjoram, Parmesan and bread crumbs; mix well.
- Divide filling among tart shells, pressing down lightly. Bake in a 350 degree oven for 20 to 25 minutes until lightly golden. Let tarts sit in the pans for 7 minutes before removing.

To freeze, bake them first, cool in pans, transfer to a baking sheet and freeze. They are best stored in a plastic container since they are fragile. Reheat in a 350 degree oven.

TOASTED MUSHROOM ROLLS

Makes 44 to 46 Pieces

½ *pound fresh mushrooms*
¼ *cup butter or margarine*
3 *tablespoons flour*
½ *teaspoon salt*
1 *cup half and half*
2 *teaspoons minced chives*
1 *teaspoon lemon juice*
22-23 *slices fresh bread*

- Clean and chop mushrooms. Heat butter or margarine; sauté mushrooms for about 5 minutes. Blend in flour, salt and half and half. Cook until thick, remove from heat, stir in minced chives and lemon juice. Let cool.

- Remove crusts from bread slices. Flatten with a rolling pin and spread with mushroom mixture. Roll up; place on a baking sheet with seam side down. When ready to serve, brush with a little melted butter or margarine.

- Bake at 400 degrees for 15 to 20 minutes or until slightly browned. Cut each roll in half and serve immediately.

These can be frozen on a baking sheet and transferred to a plastic bag. When needed, just remove the desired amount and place on a baking sheet; bake at 400 degrees until hot and brown.

HOT EGGPLANT CAVIAR

Serves 10 to 12

1 large eggplant
4 tablespoons olive oil
1 garlic clove, crushed
½ cup finely chopped onion
½ cup seeded and finely chopped green pepper
2 cups finely chopped Italian plum tomatoes
2 teaspoons capers
1 tablespoon fresh lemon juice
⅛ teaspoon red pepper sauce
1 teaspoon salt (optional)
⅛ teaspoon pepper
2 to 3 tablespoons garlic wine vinegar
1 teaspoon dried basil
½ teaspoon dried oregano
  Melba toast rounds
½ cup freshly grated Parmesan cheese

- Bake unpeeled eggplant in a shallow pan in a 350 degree oven for 1 hour. Remove from oven and cool.
- Heat olive oil in a 10 to 12-inch skillet over medium heat; add garlic, onion and green pepper. Cook until onion is tender, about 5 minutes, stirring frequently.
- Cut eggplant lengthwise; scoop out flesh, discarding skin. If there are any large pieces of eggplant, mash them with a potato ricer or cut into small pieces with a sharp knife.
- Stir eggplant into the onion mixture; add tomatoes, capers, lemon juice, red pepper sauce, salt, pepper, vinegar, basil and oregano. Simmer over low heat, uncovered, for 20 minutes.
- Remove from heat; chill a minimum of 2 hours.
- To serve, spread a heaping teaspoon of eggplant caviar on each melba toast round, sprinkle with cheese and place under a preheated broiler until bubbly, about 2 to 3 minutes. Serve at once.

AEGEAN LOAF

Serves 6 to 8

1   *loaf sourdough bread, unsliced*
5   *medium tomatoes, peeled, seeded, and finely chopped*
4   *green onions, whites only, thinly sliced*
½   *cup chopped ripe olives*
½   *cup chopped green olives with pimiento center*
4   *tablespoons chopped fresh parsley*
4   *tablespoons freshly grated Parmesan cheese*
¼   *teaspoon dried thyme*
½   *teaspoon dried oregano*
3   *tablespoons olive oil*
3   *tablespoons dry white wine*
     salt and pepper to taste

- Remove ends from bread. Using a long-handled kitchen fork, scoop out enough bread dough to make a long hollow tube with a ½-inch crust, reserving the bread crumbs.
- Combine bread crumbs, tomatoes, green onions, olives, parsley, cheese, thyme, and oregano.
- Add olive oil, white wine and salt and pepper. Thoroughly mix again.
- Holding one end of tube of sourdough bread closed with palm of your hand, stuff hollow bread with tomato mixture, being sure to pack firmly.
- Wrap stuffed loaf with aluminum foil and chill for 24 hours.
- When ready to serve, cut carefully with a very sharp knife into ½-inch slices. Serve as an appetizer on chilled small plate with fork and knife.

MEDITERRANEAN CAVIAR

Makes 3 Cups

2 tablespoons canola or olive oil
1 onion, chopped
½ cup sun-dried tomatoes, cut into thin strips
1 carrot, shredded
1 green or yellow pepper, seeded and finely chopped
1 small eggplant, peeled and minced
1 teaspoon salt
¼ teaspoon pepper
1 teaspoon sugar
1 teaspoon red wine vinegar
2 tablespoons chopped fresh cilantro
   pita bread rounds or crackers

- Heat oil in a large skillet; add onion; sauté 2 or 3 minutes.
- Stir in tomatoes, carrot, green or yellow pepper, eggplant, salt, pepper, sugar and vinegar. Simmer 15 to 20 minutes, stirring occasionally, until vegetables are tender. Stir in cilantro.
- Cut each pita round into 6 or 8 wedges. Let each person spoon vegetable mixture on pita wedges.

GORGONZOLA WALNUT ROUNDS

Makes 2 to 3 Dozen

1 narrow French bread baguette, frozen
½ cup olive oil
2 tablespoons chopped fresh basil, or 2 teaspoons dried basil
3 garlic cloves, minced
¼ pound walnuts
⅓ pound Gorgonzola cheese, crumbled
   fresh basil leaves for garnish

- Slice bread in ¼-inch slices.
- Combine olive oil, basil and 2 garlic cloves. Reserve 1 tablespoon of this mixture; brush remainder on one side of each bread round. Bake at 300 degrees until golden brown.
- In a food processor, blend walnuts, 1 garlic clove and reserved oil until mixture reaches a pastelike consistency. Spread 2 teaspoons on untoasted side of each bread round; top with crumbled cheese.
- Bake at 350 degrees until the cheese bubbles. Sprinkle with chopped basil.

Mushroom Almond Pâté

3   *tablespoons unsalted butter or margarine*
1   *onion, finely chopped*
3   *garlic cloves, finely chopped*
¾   *pound mushrooms, chopped*
½   *teaspoon thyme*
1   *cup sliced almonds, toasted*
2   *tablespoons olive oil*
¼   *cup balsamic vinegar*
¼   *teaspoon salt*
½   *teaspoon freshly ground pepper*

❧ Heat butter or margarine in a large pan. Sauté onion, garlic, mushrooms and thyme over medium low heat until soft.

❧ Process toasted almonds and olive oil in a food processor until as smooth as possible.

❧ Add mushroom mixture, vinegar, salt and pepper; process until mixture becomes very smooth.

❧ Transfer to a serving bowl and refrigerate, covered, several hours.

❧ Serve with light rye bread, crackers and grapes, pears and Brie cheese.

This interesting combination of ingredients will intrigue your guests!

Spicy Walnut Spread

2   *cups fine fresh French bread crumbs*
2   *cups finely chopped walnuts*
1½   *teaspoons cumin*
1½   *teaspoons paprika*
¼   *cup fresh lemon juice*
½   *teaspoon cayenne*
2   *tablespoons vegetable oil*

❧ Mix all ingredients and chill.
❧ Serve with Armenian cracker bread or crackers.

POTATO SALAD APPETIZERS

Serves 6

15   small red new potatoes
 1   tablespoon olive oil
½   teaspoon salt, divided
¼   teaspoon freshly ground black pepper, divided
¼   cup mayonnaise
¼   cup sour cream
⅛   teaspoon garlic powder
 2   tablespoons finely minced celery
 2   teaspoons country-style Dijon mustard
 1   teaspoon lemon juice
½   teaspoon crushed dried dill
 4   drops red pepper sauce
      lettuce leaves, any variety
15   green olives stuffed with pimiento, cut in halves

- Scrub potatoes but do not peel; cut in half.
- Toss potatoes with olive oil, ¼ teaspoon salt and ⅛ teaspoon pepper. Arrange in a single layer in a large baking pan and bake in a 350 degree oven for 50 minutes or until tender when pierced. Remove from oven, cool, cover and refrigerate. (May be done 24 hours in advance.)
- Stir together mayonnaise, sour cream, garlic powder, celery, mustard, lemon juice, dill, hot pepper sauce and remaining ¼ teaspoon salt and ⅛ teaspoon pepper. Cover and refrigerate up to 12 hours.
- Arrange the lettuce leaves on a large platter; top with potatoes. Spoon about ½ teaspoon of the dressing on top of each potato half, garnish with a green olive half, cut side up. Cover loosely; refrigerate up to 4 hours.

Make this dish entirely ahead of time! It also doubles as an elegant side dish on a cold buffet!

HOT TOMATOES

Serves 8 to 10

40   cherry tomatoes
 1   4-ounce can green chilies, chopped
⅔   cup diced celery
 3   tablespoons chopped green onion or Walla Walla Sweets
 3   tablespoons wine vinegar
 1   teaspoon sugar

- Core tomatoes and set aside.
- Mix remaining ingredients and stuff tomatoes. Chill and serve.

MARINATED BRUSSELS SPROUTS

Serves 6 to 8

1½   pounds Brussels sprouts
1½   teaspoons finely minced onion
 1   cup tomato sauce
 1   garlic clove, crushed
 1   teaspoon sugar
     pinch cayenne pepper
1½   teaspoons olive oil
2½   tablespoons dill or tarragon vinegar
 1   large bay leaf

- Wash Brussels sprouts, trim bases and remove any discolored outer leaves. Pierce base of each sprout with a small knife so they will cook evenly.
- Bring 1½ quarts of water to a boil; add sprouts, remove from heat and allow to cool.
- Combine remaining ingredients. Add sprouts.
- Refrigerate marinated sprouts for 24 hours. Remove bay leaf from marinade before serving.

An excellent addition to an antipasto tray.

ROASTED PEPPER SPREAD

Makes One Cup

   1   7-ounce jar roasted red peppers, drained
1 to 2   jalapeño chilies, seeded
   4   large green olives, pitted
   1   tablespoon fresh parsley
   2   teaspoons olive oil
1½   teaspoons fresh lemon juice
     salt and pepper to taste
     French bread or sesame crackers

- In a food processor, finely chop the peppers, chilies, olives and parsley. Add olive oil and lemon juice; process just until mixed. Add salt and pepper.
- Spread on French bread slices or sesame crackers.

MINIATURE SPINACH FRITTATAS

Makes 18

vegetable cooking spray

½ 10-ounce package frozen chopped spinach, thawed
    and squeezed dry

¾ cup Ricotta cheese

½ cup grated Parmesan or Asiago cheese

½ cup chopped mushrooms

2 tablespoons chopped onion

½ teaspoon oregano

¼ teaspoon black pepper

1 egg

- Coat 18 miniature muffin cups with cooking spray.
- Combine spinach, cheeses, mushrooms, onion, oregano and pepper. Beat in egg.
- Spoon two tablespoons of mixture into each muffin cup. Bake 20 to 25 minutes until firm.
- Serve 3 on a plate and garnish with a sprig of fresh oregano and a cherry tomato.

*Good either hot or cold and may
also be used as a vegetable dish*

DATES MOROCCAN

Serves 6

¾ cup brown sugar

½ cup water

⅓ cup lemon juice

¼ cup cider vinegar

1 teaspoon grated orange rind

½ teaspoon cinnamon

¼ teaspoon nutmeg

⅛ teaspoon salt

8 to 12 ounces pitted dates

- Combine all ingredients except dates in sauce pan. Bring to boil; cook, stirring, until sugar dissolves. Reduce heat and simmer 5 minutes.
- Place dates in bowl and pour spice mixture over them; let cool. Refrigerate 24 to 48 hours.
- Serve at room temperature using toothpicks or appetizer forks.
- Variation: Drain dates. Wrap in ½ slice of bacon; skewer with toothpick. Broil until bacon is crisp. Best served while still warm.

*Full of the flavors of the Middle
East.*

RAISIN CURRY SLICES

Makes About 36 Appetizers

2   *tablespoons butter or margarine*
4   *teaspoons curry powder*
⅔   *cup finely chopped onion*
2   *cups finely chopped seedless raisins*
⅔   *cup dry sherry*
1   *recipe for pie pastry or 1 package pastry mix*

- In small saucepan heat butter with curry powder; add onion and cook slightly; add raisins and sherry. Cover pan and simmer 5 to 10 minutes until liquid is absorbed; cool.
- Prepare pastry; divide in half and roll out each piece to a 9x10½-inch rectangle. Spread half of cooled raisin mixture on each piece of pastry. Roll up from long side, to make two 10½-inch rolls, pinching edges to seal.
- Bake on ungreased baking sheet at 375 degrees for 25 to 30 minutes until brown. Cool and cut into slices.

Easy to put together. Serve with very crisp white wine!

CRAB CLOUDS

Serves 6

1   *teaspoon olive oil*
6   *green onions, shredded diagonally*
1   *cup cooked crab, broken in small pieces*
6   *mushrooms, sliced*
1½   *teaspoon green peppercorns*
2   *large egg whites*
2   *teaspoons grated Pecorino or Parmesan cheese*
1   *7-ounce can minced clams, drained*

- Oil 6 small (½ cup) soufflé dishes; line with shredded onions to make grassy little nests.
- Divide crab, mushrooms and green peppercorns evenly among dishes.
- Beat egg whites until stiff; fold in grated cheese and minced clams. Spoon over crab; broil for 3 to 5 minutes until golden brown. Serve hot.

Use 12 tiny fluted pastry shells instead of soufflé dishes, or cook entire recipe in a 2-quart baking dish as an entree.

COLD MUSSELS WITH RED PEPPER RELISH

Serves 6 to 8

2 pounds mussels, unshelled
½ cup dry white wine
1½ tablespoons unsalted butter
⅓ cup finely chopped red onions
2 tablespoons minced green onions
½ cup finely chopped red bell peppers
2 teaspoons cider vinegar
2 teaspoons sugar
¼ teaspoon freshly ground black pepper

🍃 Place mussels and wine in a large shallow pan with a lid. Cook, covered, over high heat for 5 to 8 minutes, or until the shells open.

🍃 Transfer mussels to a jelly-roll pan, discarding any unopened shells. Discard top shells and release mussels from bottom shells, leaving them in the shells.

🍃 Chill mussels, loosely covered with damp paper towels, at least 2 hours or overnight.

🍃 Heat butter in a skillet. Add red and green onions and cook until limp, about 5 minutes. Add red peppers and steam, covered, for 3 minutes. Add vinegar and sugar; cook 1 minute.

🍃 Add black and cayenne peppers, stir and cook for 1 more minute. Remove from heat; chill until ready to serve.

🍃 To serve, arrange mussels on a large platter or divide among 6 plates. Carefully spoon 1 teaspoon of the relish on each mussel.

SESAME CHICKEN NUGGETS

Serves 4 to 5

⅓ cup unseasoned bread crumbs
2   tablespoons sesame seeds
2   tablespoons grated Parmesan cheese
12 ounces chicken breasts, boned and skinned
2   egg whites, beaten
½   tablespoon olive oil

Yogurt Honey Mustard
½   cup low-fat plain yogurt
1½ teaspoons honey
2   teaspoons prepared mustard

- Combine bread crumbs, sesame seed and Parmesan cheese in a small bowl.
- Cut chicken breasts into 1½-inch pieces. Dip the chicken pieces in beaten egg whites, then in the crumb mixture.
- Spray a 13x9-inch baking dish with cooking spray. Arrange chicken in pan and sprinkle with olive oil.
- Bake at 425 degrees for 15 minutes, or until cooked, turning the nuggets once.
- Combine sauce ingredients. Serve with chicken nuggets.

This is a "kid-tested" recipe. They can make it and will eat it! Try this recipe with Arboretum Honey from our gift shop.

BAKED CORN CHIPS

Makes 8 Cups

20 corn tortillas
    margarine, not more than 2 teaspoons

- Scrape each tortilla with a small amount of soft margarine. Cut tortillas, several at a time, into 8 pie-shaped wedges using kitchen shears. Arrange in a single layer on cookie sheet.
- Bake at 350 degrees until crisp and slightly browned, about 10 minutes. Store in an airtight container.

QUESADILLA

12 medium flour tortillas
¼ cup unsalted butter, melted
¾ cup tomatillo sauce (fresh or bottled)
1 pound Monterey Jack cheese, grated
½ cup chopped fresh cilantro
¼ cup finely grated Parmesan cheese

- Place 1 tortilla on a buttered cookie sheet; brush with butter. Top with some sauce, Jack cheese and cilantro. Repeat for 2 more layers. Top with a tortilla, brush with butter, and sprinkle with Parmesan cheese.
- Repeat the entire procedure using the remaining tortillas to make 3 stacks.
- Bake at 350 degrees for 10 minutes, or until lightly browned. Cut each stack in 8 wedges and serve immediately.

MEDITERRANEAN TOAST

6 French bread slices
¼ cup olive oil
½ teaspoon garlic powder
1 tablespoon chopped fresh parsley
½ teaspoon dried oregano leaves
1 teaspoon toasted sesame seeds
¼ teaspoon paprika

- Place bread slices on baking sheet.
- In a small bowl thoroughly combine remaining ingredients. Brush each slice of bread with mixture.
- Place under broiler and brown; turn slices and brush again. Return to broiler. Toast until brown. Serve at once.

Once you've tasted this, you'll prefer it to buttered toast.

PICNIC PÂTÉ

1   *cup coarsely chopped carrots*
2   *medium onions, cut in eighths*
4   *large garlic cloves*
½   *cup parsley sprigs*
2½   *teaspoons thyme*
1   *teaspoon freshly ground black pepper*
1   *teaspoon salt*
2   *pounds finely ground lean beef round or chuck*
1   *pound finely ground pork shoulder*
1   *cup fresh bread crumbs*
2   *eggs, lightly beaten or 4 egg whites*
1   *cup orzo or other very small pasta, cooked and drained*
6   *bacon strips*

- Process carrots, onions, garlic, parsley, thyme, pepper and salt in food processor until finely chopped, about 30 seconds.
- Put mixture into a large bowl and add beef, pork, bread crumbs, eggs and pasta. Mix well with hands.
- Form mixture into a firm oval loaf. In a shallow baking pan, lay 3 of the bacon strips lengthwise. Place the loaf on top of the bacon and lay the remaining bacon across the top of the loaf.
- Bake in a preheated 350 degree oven for 1½ hours or until done. Serve hot or cold.

Great to take along for a picnic or tailgate party. Truly sinful!

SOUPS

BORDER BEAN POT

2   cups dried pinto beans
1   pound ham, cubed, plus a ham hock for flavor
1   quart water
1   22-ounce can tomato juice
4   cups chicken stock
3   onions, chopped
3   garlic cloves, minced
3   tablespoons chopped fresh parsley
¼   cup chopped green pepper
4   tablespoons brown sugar
1   tablespoon chili powder
1   teaspoon salt or to taste
3   whole bay leaves
1   tablespoon oregano
½   teaspoon ground cumin seeds
½   teaspoon dried rosemary leaves, crushed
½   teaspoon celery seed
½   teaspoon thyme
½   teaspoon ground marjoram
½   teaspoon sweet basil, crushed
¼   teaspoon curry powder
4   whole cloves
1   cup sherry or red wine

- Cover beans with water and soak overnight. Drain and discard water. Add all other ingredients except sherry. Bring to a boil. Lower heat and simmer until beans are tender, about 2 to 2½ hours.
- Remove cloves and bay leaves. Add sherry or red wine. Serve in soup bowls; top with chopped green onion.

Surpasses even our local favorite "mixed bean" recipes. Try this for a special treat! Freezes well, too.

Add cider vinegar to sparkle up soups, etc., rather than more salt.

CHIOPPINO

2   medium onions, chopped

1   large green pepper, seeded and cut into strips

¼   cup olive oil

2   teaspoons salt or to taste

¼   teaspoon pepper

2   garlic cloves, minced

1   28-ounce can crushed tomatoes

2   cups red wine

2   teaspoons marjoram

2   teaspoons sweet basil

½   teaspoon rosemary

1   teaspoon thyme

2   dozen steamer clams in the shell, scrubbed

1   cup crab meat

1   pound halibut fillets, cut in chunks

½   pound prawns

½   pound scallops

¼   cup parsley, snipped

- Sauté onion and green pepper in olive oil in large pan. Add remaining ingredients except clams, crab, halibut, prawns, scallops and parsley. Cook 10 minutes.
- Add fish and clams; simmer 20 minutes. Sprinkle with parsley before serving.

TUNA JACK CHOWDER

Serves 4

4   tablespoons butter or margarine
¼   cup chopped celery
1   cup chopped onion
2   cups diced potato
1¼   teaspoon salt or to taste
¼   teaspoon white pepper
½   teaspoon thyme
½   teaspoon dill weed
2   tablespoons flour
3   cups milk
1   cup stewed tomatoes
1   6½-ounce can tuna, drained
1   cup grated Monterey Jack cheese
2   tablespoons minced parsley

❧ Heat 2 tablespoons butter in dutch oven; add celery, onion and potato. Cook 15 minutes or until potato is tender, stirring often. Add salt, pepper, thyme and dill weed.

❧ Blend flour with ¼ cup of milk; add to remaining milk and combine with cooked vegetables. Add tomatoes and tuna. Heat and stir until soup is thickened. Stir in cheese, parsley and remaining 2 tablespoons of margarine or butter.

GARLIC PIPERADE SOUP

Serves 4

20   garlic cloves
2   green onions, sliced
1   green pepper, sliced
2   cups beef broth, divided
3   cups chopped ripe tomatoes
        salt and pepper to taste

❧ Blanch garlic cloves 30 seconds in boiling water. Rinse under cold water. Drain, peel and slice.

❧ Sauté onion and green pepper in 2 to 3 tablespoons of the broth until they become golden, about 15 minutes. Add garlic, tomatoes, remaining broth and season with salt and pepper. Heat and serve.

A surprisingly light and tasty soup that has an extremely subtle garlic flavor.

"BETTER THAN" OYSTER STEW

Serves 4 to 5

1   tablespoon chopped onion
2   tablespoons chopped pimiento
1   tablespoon chopped parsley
2   cups water
⅓   cup margarine
1   10-ounce jar of medium oysters, cut into bite-size
    pieces
4   tablespoons flour
4   cups milk
½   teaspoon salt or to taste

- Simmer onion, pimiento and parsley in 2 cups water in large covered pan for 25 minutes. Cool and put through blender.
- Heat margarine and sauté oysters briefly.
- Blend flour with small amount of milk. Add remaining milk, stirring until smooth.
- Combine all ingredients and add salt, if desired. Heat, stirring often, until mixture thickens. Don't overcook oysters!

ELEGANT TURKEY SOUP

Serves 8

½   cup chopped onion
1   garlic clove, minced
1   small jalapeno pepper, minced
2   tablespoons vegetable oil
5   cups turkey or chicken broth
2   cups cooked turkey, cubed
1½ pounds sweet potato, peeled and cut into ½-inch
    cubes
1   tablespoon vinegar
1½ cups frozen corn
1   teaspoon salt or to taste
2   drops red pepper sauce
2   tablespoons finely cut fresh cilantro for garnish

- Sauté onion, garlic and jalapeño pepper in hot oil in large saucepan. Add broth, turkey and cubed sweet potatoes. Cook until potatoes are tender. Add vinegar, corn, salt and red pepper sauce. Stir in cilantro.
- Serve when corn is tender. Garnish with additional cilantro.

Unusual ingredients make this soup outstanding.

CLAM CHOWDER

3   tablespoons margarine
1   cup chopped onion
1   garlic clove, minced
4   slices bacon, cooked, drained and crumbled
3   cups chicken stock or 2 cans chicken broth
2½ cups diced baking potatoes
1   bay leaf
¼   teaspoon thyme
⅛   teaspoon allspice
¼   teaspoon black pepper
1   cup bottled clam juice
1½ cups milk (part canned condensed milk adds a
    rich flavor)
3   tablespoons flour
3   tablespoons milk
3   dozen clams, steamed open and chopped or 3 cans
    chopped clams
    paprika
    slivered green onions

🍂 Heat margarine in dutch oven; sauté onion and garlic until soft. Add bacon, stock, potatoes, bay leaf, thyme, allspice and pepper; cover and bring to a boil. Lower heat and simmer 10 minutes or until potatoes are cooked.

🍂 Remove bay leaf. Add clam juice and 1½ cups milk; heat without boiling.

🍂 Mix flour and 3 tablespoons milk to form a paste and add to soup. Heat and stir to thicken. Add minced clams; adjust seasonings and serve hot. Sprinkle each serving with paprika and slivered green onions.

SUPER SUPPER SOUP

Serves 6 to 8

1   *medium onion, chopped*
2   *tablespoons salad oil*
1   *pound lean ground round*
1   *14-ounce can stewed tomatoes*
3   *14-ounce cans beef broth*
1   *large eggplant, unpeeled and diced*
½   *cup sliced carrots*
½   *cup sliced celery*
½   *cup sliced fresh mushrooms*
1   *teaspoon salt or to taste*
1   *teaspoon sugar*
½   *teaspoon pepper*
½   *teaspoon nutmeg*
1   *tablespoon cider vinegar*
½   *cup uncooked salad macaroni*
    Parmesan cheese

- In large saucepan, sauté onion in salad oil until limp; add ground round and continue cooking until beef is no longer pink. Remove fat.
- Add remaining ingredients except macaroni. Simmer 30 minutes or until vegetables are tender. Add macaroni. Simmer another 15 minutes or until macaroni is cooked.
- Serve with Parmesan cheese sprinkled on top.

*Crusty rolls are a great
accompaniment for this soup.*

HOT TOMATO SMOOTHIE

Serves 5 to 6

1   tablespoon butter or margarine
1   medium onion, sliced
1   16-ounce can tomatoes or equivalent of fresh
    tomato
2   cups regular strength chicken broth
    pinch ground cloves
½   teaspoon dried basil
1   teaspoon nutmeg
1   teaspoon black pepper
2   tablespoons minced parsley
1   bay leaf
1   teaspoon paprika
1   teaspoon sugar

- Combine all ingredients. Simmer for 30 minutes.
- Remove bay leaf and process in food processor.
  Serve hot.

This soup will warm your soul on a cold day. The addition of ½ cup cream creates a different tasting soup.

GOLDEN BROCCOLI SOUP

Serves 8

2   2-pound bags frozen chopped broccoli or an equal
    amount of fresh chopped broccoli
2   14½-ounce cans chicken broth
1   medium onion, quartered
2   tablespoons margarine
½   teaspoon salt or to taste
    freshly ground pepper to taste
1   teaspoon curry powder or to taste
2   tablespoons lime juice
1   tablespoon per serving of sour cream or plain
    yogurt
1   lemon, sliced

- Combine all ingredients except sour cream or yogurt
  and lemon in a large pot and cook, stirring
  occasionally, over medium heat for 12 minutes.
- Purée in blender or food processor. Garnish each
  serving with sour cream or yogurt and a slice of
  lemon.

Good cold or hot.

UKRAINIAN BORSCH

Serves 8 to 10

1 *pound beef chuck with bone in, or*
1 *pound lean beef stew meat plus 2 marrow bones*
3 *14-ounce cans beef broth*
1 *bay leaf*
10 *whole allspice*
1 *tablespoon salt or to taste*
3 *tablespoons cider vinegar*
2 *carrots, sliced*
1 *medium onion, chopped*
1 *cup sliced celery*
2 *16-ounce cans beets, or 4 to 6 fresh beets, cut in strips*
4 *cups shredded cabbage*
2 *cups diced potatoes*
1 *6-ounce can tomato paste*
1 *16-ounce carton sour cream*
    dillweed

◆ Put beef in large kettle. Add 4 cups water and bring to a full boil. Skim froth. Add beef broth, bay leaf, whole allspice, salt and cider vinegar. Simmer for 30 minutes.

◆ Add carrots, onion, celery, shredded beets, shredded cabbage, diced, peeled potatoes and tomato paste. Simmer 1½ hours.

◆ Discard bay leaf and allspice. Remove meat and cut into bite-size pieces. Return to soup pot. Season to taste. Serve topped with a dollop of sour cream and a sprinkle of dillweed.

Foccacio bread, brushed with olive oil, sprinkled with garlic salt and heated at 300 degrees for 20 minutes and an avocado salad served with this soup would make a delicious supper.

Use a tea strainer in the soup pot to package small spices such as cloves, peppercorns and allspice for easy removal later.

CREAM OF CAULIFLOWER SOUP

Serves 8 to 10

1 large head of cauliflower
3 stalks of celery, finely minced
2 tablespoons chopped onion
4 tablespoons butter or margarine
4 cups chicken broth
4 tablespoons flour
1 cup whole milk
1 cup buttermilk
1 teaspoon curry powder
2 tablespoons chicken bouillon
   salt and white pepper to taste
   Swiss cheese (optional)
   paprika

- Separate cauliflower into florets and slice the stalks. Set aside a few florets to add to soup for garnish. Cook remaining cauliflower in 1 cup of water. Cool slightly; then purée in blender with the cooking liquid. Put puréed soup in large saucepan.

- Sauté celery and onion in melted butter or margarine until soft; add to saucepan.

- Add chicken broth, less 4 tablespoons, to saucepan. Mix remaining broth with 4 tablespoons of flour to make a paste; slowly add mixture to soup, stirring carefully. Cook, stirring, until smooth and thickened.

- Add milk, buttermilk, curry and chicken bouillon to soup. Season to taste.

- Garnish with reserved florets. Serve with grated Swiss cheese, if desired, and paprika.

SUMMER SALAD SOUP

Serves 4 to 5

1 pint plain low fat yogurt
1 10½-ounce can condensed chicken broth
1 cup pitted ripe olives, sliced
½ cup unpeeled cucumber sliced paper-thin and
   quartered
¼ cup sliced green onion
¼ cup chopped green pepper
1 tablespoon minced parsley
½ teaspoon pepper

- Blend yogurt and chicken broth in blender or food processor. Stir in remaining ingredients.

- Chill at least 2 hours. Garnish with additional olive slices.

Refreshing on a warm summer evening. Serve before grilled fish and fresh corn on the cob.

CREAMY MUSHROOM SOUP

Serves 8

2   cups chopped onions
2   tablespoons minced garlic
2   tablespoons vegetable oil
¼   cup uncooked pearl barley
¼   teaspoon ground nutmeg
1½ pounds white mushrooms
8   cups chicken broth
¼   cup sherry
½   cup chopped flat-leafed parsley
    salt and white pepper to taste

- Sauté onion and garlic in oil over medium low heat in a large pot. Add uncooked barley and nutmeg. Cook for 1 minute, stirring.
- Reserve six mushrooms for garnish. Chop remainder and add with chicken broth and sherry to soup. Bring to a boil, reduce heat and simmer for 40 minutes. Add parsley.
- Cool soup slightly. Purée in batches in a blender or food processor. Return to pot. Season with salt and pepper. Warm soup gently. Garnish individual bowls of soup with thinly sliced mushrooms and additional minced parsley.

The barley enriches the soup so you have a creamy soup without any cream!

PURÉE OF SWEET PEPPER SOUP

Serves 6

5   large red bell peppers, seeded and cut in 1-inch pieces
3   14½-ounce cans chicken broth
1   medium red onion, cut into 1-inch cubes
1   large potato, peeled and cut into 1-inch cubes
½   teaspoon crumbled dried thyme
2   bay leaves
1   whole clove
    salt and pepper to taste
    sour cream or plain yogurt for garnish

- In heavy saucepan, combine peppers, chicken broth, onion and potato. Cover and simmer 45 minutes over medium heat. Strain the vegetables, reserving stock.
- Purée vegetables with 1 cup of broth in blender or food processor. Add 1 more cup of broth and strain into saucepan to remove fine rolls of red pepper skin. Add remaining broth.
- Tie clove, bay leaves and thyme in cheesecloth square, or use a tea strainer, and add to soup. Season with salt and pepper. Simmer 25 minutes, stirring occasionally.
- Discard herbs. Chill soup several hours. Serve with a dollop of sour cream or yogurt.

SI SI CORN CHOWDER

Serves 8 to 10

8   slices bacon
1   tablespoon olive oil
1   medium onion, chopped
4   garlic cloves, minced
2   large stalks celery, chopped
1   green or red pepper, chopped
1   4-ounce can chopped mild chilies
1   4-ounce jar diced pimiento
3   cups whole kernel corn, fresh or frozen
4   tablespoons flour
4   tablespoons melted butter or margarine
6   cups milk
1   cup finely diced ham
1   teaspoon chopped dried cilantro or 1 tablespoon
     chopped fresh cilantro
⅔ teaspoon red pepper flakes
1   teaspoon cumin
1   teaspoon ground coriander
     salt to taste

- Sauté bacon, crumble and set aside. Reserve 1 tablespoon of bacon fat and add olive oil, onion, garlic, celery, green or red pepper and sauté slowly.
- Add chilies, pimiento and corn; add flour and melted butter and blend until mixture forms a thick paste.
- Add milk, ham and seasonings; simmer slowly a few minutes to blend flavors.

The flavor blends are superb! Don't eliminate any ingredients until you try it this way once.

SALADS

CHICKEN SALAD WITH APRICOTS AND AVOCADO *Serves 4*

3 cups cubed cooked chicken
1½ cups unpeeled and pitted fresh apricots
⅓ cup thinly sliced celery
¼ cup thinly sliced green onions
⅓ cup mayonnaise
⅓ cup sour cream or yogurt
1 tablespoon dry vermouth
½ teaspoon grated lemon rind
  dash nutmeg or ginger
1 avocado, peeled, seeded and sliced
1 tablespoon lime or lemon juice
  Boston or Butter lettuce
⅓ cup sliced almonds

- Lightly mix chicken, apricots, celery and onion.
- In a small bowl, mix mayonnaise, sour cream or yogurt, vermouth, lemon rind and nutmeg or ginger until smooth. Combine with chicken mixture, mixing lightly until well coated. Cover and refrigerate for 1 to 3 hours to blend flavors.
- Brush avocado slices well on all sides with lime or lemon juice.
- Line 4 plates with lettuce leaves; divide chicken mixture among the plates. Garnish each serving with a fourth of the avocado slices. Sprinkle with almonds.

If fresh apricots are not available, try moist-packed dried apricots. And try substituting red apples for avocados.

HOT SEAFOOD SALAD

Serves 8

1   cup white fish, cooked and flaked or 1 can tuna, drained

1   cup shrimp, crab or scallops, cooked

1   red or yellow pepper, finely chopped

½   cup finely chopped onion

½   cup finely chopped celery

1   cup toasted bread crumbs

1   cup low-fat cottage cheese

2   tablespoons lemon juice

1½   teaspoons Worcestershire sauce

½   cup grated mozzarella, Asiago or Romano cheese

½   cup slivered almonds
    paprika for garnish

- Combine all ingredients except paprika and put into a 1½-quart baking dish. Sprinkle with paprika.
- Bake at 350 degrees for 25 to 30 minutes.

SALMON PASTA SALAD

Serves 4 to 6

½   pound small pasta shells

¼   pound green beans

1   pound cooked salmon, broken into small chunks
    lettuce

Cottage Cheese and Yogurt Dressing

½   cup low-fat cottage cheese

½   cup low-fat yogurt

1   tablespoon lemon juice

½   cup coarsely chopped fresh dill
    freshly ground black pepper to taste

- Cook pasta in boiling water. Drain and rinse well.
- Cut green beans into 1½-inch lengths and blanch in boiling water for 2 minutes. Drain and set aside.
- To make dressing, purée cottage cheese using a food processor or a sieve; combine with yogurt, lemon juice, dill and pepper.
- Mix pasta, beans, salmon and dressing. Serve on lettuce leaves.

TUNA SALAD WITH ORIENTAL-STYLE DRESSING   *Serves 2*

1   *6½-ounce can tuna, drained well and flaked*
½   *cucumber, peeled, halved lengthwise, seeded, and thinly sliced crosswise*
6   *cherry tomatoes, halved*
½   *red bell pepper, diced*
2   *green onions*
¼   *pound snow peas, trimmed, blanched for 30 seconds, and plunged into ice water and drained*
½   *cup mung bean sprouts, rinsed and drained well lettuce leaves for lining the plates, if desired*

Dressing

1½   *tablespoons soy sauce*
2½   *tablespoons rice vinegar*
1   *teaspoon sesame oil*
1   *teaspoon sesame seeds, toasted lightly*
¼   *teaspoon sugar*
   salt and freshly ground black pepper to taste

- In a large bowl, combine tuna, cucumber, tomatoes, bell pepper, green onions, snow peas and bean sprouts.
- Whisk together all ingredients for dressing.
- Toss the tuna mixture with the dressing and divide the salad between 2 plates lined with lettuce.

STEVE'S REPUBLICAN BARBECUED STEAK SALAD

1½   pounds top round steak, cut 1 inch thick
6   cups assorted crisp greens
2   6-ounce jars marinated artichoke hearts
3   Roma tomatoes, chopped
1   red pepper, chopped
1   bunch green onions, chopped
4-6   ounces Italian-style salad dressing

- Barbecue meat to medium rare.
- Cool and cut into thin slices.
- Clean and tear greens into small pieces.
- Drain artichokes and cut into halves.
- Toss all together ½ hour before serving.

SPINACH AND SMOKED TURKEY PASTA SALAD

Serves 8

8   ounces penne
½   cup chopped fresh parsley
½   teaspoon dried oregano
1   teaspoon dried basil
1   garlic clove, pressed
½   cup red wine vinegar
⅓   cup olive oil
2   teaspoons sugar
1   tablespoon Dijon mustard
6   ounces smoked turkey breast, cut into small pieces
1   small red onion, chopped
1   red bell pepper, cut into thin strips
6   ounces sliced provolone cheese, cut in small
     narrow pieces
1   medium zucchini, cut into thin strips
1   bunch fresh spinach
     salt and pepper to taste

- Cook penne and cool.
- Combine parsley, oregano, basil, garlic, vinegar, olive oil, sugar and mustard; blend in blender or food processor. Mix with cooked penne, turkey, onion, red pepper, cheese and zucchini. Add salt and pepper.
- Refrigerate for at least 30 minutes.
- Wash, pat dry and tear spinach into bite size pieces.
- Just before serving, toss refrigerated mixture with spinach.

A full meal! Good salad for picnics and potlucks.

SMOKED TURKEY AND WILD RICE SALAD

Serves 6

1   cup uncooked wild rice
1   14-ounce can regular strength chicken broth
1   pound smoked turkey
3   Roma tomatoes, cubed
2   cups chopped celery
¼   cup chopped green onions with tops
2   tablespoons chopped pimiento
½   cup vegetable oil
¼   cup red wine vinegar
    salt and pepper to taste
2   medium avocados, chopped
1   tablespoon lemon juice

🍃 Cook wild rice as directed on box, except use chicken broth for part of the liquid.

🍃 Mix cooked wild rice, smoked turkey, tomatoes, celery, green onions and pimiento; cover and refrigerate overnight.

🍃 Mix together vegetable oil, red wine vinegar and salt and pepper; add to rice mixture.

🍃 Before serving, sprinkle part of the lemon juice on avocados to prevent darkening and mix remainder, along with avocados, into salad.

Colorful, good, substantial but not heavy. A great summer dinner!

BRITTANY ASPARAGUS VINAIGRETTE

Serves 6

2½   pounds asparagus
1   14-ounce can regular strength chicken broth
2   tablespoons white wine vinegar
2   tablespoons lemon juice
     salt to taste
½   teaspoon dry mustard
½   cup olive oil or salad oil
⅛   teaspoon pepper
⅛   teaspoon tarragon
1   hard-cooked egg, finely chopped

🍃 Break off asparagus ends and discard; wash well.

🍃 Heat broth to boiling in skillet; add asparagus and cook, uncovered, until tender when pierced, about 5 to 7 minutes. Drain. Reserve broth for other uses.

🍃 Blend vinegar, lemon juice, salt, mustard, oil, pepper and tarragon in a small bowl.

🍃 Arrange asparagus spears in 6 shallow dishes; spoon dressing over each; garnish with egg. Serve at room temperature.

CANTALOUPE AND SHRIMP BOWL

Serves 4 to 6

2   *medium-sized cantaloupe*
1   *cucumber*
½   *cup sliced celery*
¾   *pound cooked and shelled small shrimp*
      Butter lettuce
¾   *cup chopped macadamia nuts or toasted slivered*
      almonds

Lemon Dressing

¼   *cup mayonnaise*
¼   *cup sour cream*
2   *teaspoons lemon juice*
1   *teaspoon prepared horseradish*
1   *teaspoon Dijon mustard*
1   *teaspoon grated lemon peel*
¼   *teaspoon salt or to taste*
¼   *teaspoon ground cumin*

- Cut cantaloupe in half and scoop out the seeds. Use a melon ball cutter to scoop fruit into balls. Thinly slice the cucumber.
- Mix together the melon balls, cucumber, celery and shrimp.
- Line a salad bowl with lettuce leaves and spoon in the salad.
- Mix all ingredients for lemon dressing and pass at table along with nuts.

AVOCADO AND JÍCAMA SALAD

Serves 6 to 8

3 *large avocados, diced*
   juice of 2 lemons
2 *large tomatoes, chopped*
2 *cups diced jícama*
8 *ounces feta cheese, crumbled*
4 *ounces pitted ripe black olives, sliced*
4 *tablespoons olive oil*

- Arrange avocados on a serving platter in a single layer. Sprinkle a third of the lemon juice over avocados.
- Arrange tomatoes on top of avocados.
- Layer jícama over the tomatoes. Sprinkle with half of remaining lemon juice. Crumble cheese over all.
- Top with olives and sprinkle remaining lemon juice over olives and drizzle with olive oil.

Make this salad 4 to 6 hours ahead, refrigerate, and enjoy your dinner party!

AVOCADO AND GRAPEFRUIT SALAD WITH SPICY HONEY DRESSING

Serves 2

1 *grapefruit*
1 *firm ripe avocado, pitted, peeled and sliced lengthwise*
4 *soft-leafed lettuce leaves such as Boston or Bibb, rinsed and dried*

Spicy Honey Dressing
1 *tablespoon white wine vinegar*
1 *teaspoon honey*
   generous pinch of cayenne or to taste
2 *tablespoons vegetable oil*
   salt and pepper to taste

- Cut away zest and pith from grapefruit. Cut flesh into sections, reserving 1 tablespoon of juice for dressing.
- Pit and peel avocado; slice lengthwise.
- In a small bowl, whisk together dressing ingredients including 1 tablespoon of grapefruit juice.
- Arrange lettuce leaves on plates; then arrange the grapefruit sections alternately with the avocado.
- Drizzle with dressing and serve.

CITRUS TOSS-UP

1   *large head lettuce, washed and torn into bite-size pieces*
1   *cup canned mandarin oranges, drained*
½   *Walla Walla sweet onion, thinly sliced*

Sesame Mustard Dressing

1   *cup oil*
4   *tablespoons tarragon vinegar*
½   *cup sugar*
1   *teaspoon salt*
1   *tablespoon toasted sesame seeds*
1   *teaspoon dry mustard*
1   *teaspoon celery salt*
1   *tablespoon grated onion*

- Mix salad ingredients in large bowl.
- Mix dressing ingredients; combine half with salad ingredients and serve.
- Reserve the remaining dressing for another night.

Optional ingredients might be sliced mushrooms, pink grapefruit sections, fresh shrimp or marinated artichoke hearts.

BLACK BEAN WITH SWEET PEPPER AND FETA SALAD   *Serves 8*

1   *cup black beans, soaked overnight and drained*
4   *cups water*
1   *medium red bell pepper, seeded and finely diced*
1   *medium green bell pepper, seeded and finely diced*
1   *medium yellow bell pepper, seeded and finely diced*
¼   *cup finely minced red onion*
¼   *cup finely chopped fresh parsley*
½   *cup coarsely crumbled feta cheese*

Dressing
5   *tablespoons balsamic vinegar, divided*
1   *small clove garlic, peeled and finely minced*
2   *teaspoons Dijon mustard*
1   *teaspoon dried oregano, crushed*
½   *teaspoon salt or to taste*
¼   *teaspoon freshly ground black pepper*
⅓   *cup olive oil*

❧ In a large saucepan, combine black beans and water. Bring to a boil, reduce heat and simmer for 30 minutes, or until tender. Drain and rinse briefly. Set aside.

❧ Combine red, green and yellow bell peppers with red onion and parsley. Refrigerate.

❧ Prepare dressing by combining 4 tablespoons of vinegar, garlic, mustard, oregano, salt and pepper in a food processor or blender. Blend well. Drizzle in the olive oil and process until blended and thickened. Pour half of dressing over the beans and marinate at room temperature for 1 hour.

❧ Combine beans with remaining dressing and vegetables. Marinate for at least 1 hour in refrigerator to blend flavors.

❧ One-half hour before serving, remove salad from the refrigerator. Stir in remaining tablespoon of vinegar and feta cheese.

MARINATED CUCUMBER SALAD

Serves 4

2   medium cucumbers, sliced
1   large carrot, grated
¼   cup sliced green onions

- Combine vegetables in bowl.
- Mix dressing and pour over vegetables. Refrigerate at least 2 hours before serving.

Dressing

½   cup rice vinegar
¼   cup water
1   tablespoon soy sauce
1   teaspoon sugar
1   tablespoon grated fresh ginger

GREEN BEAN, WALNUT AND FETA SALAD

Serves 6

1½   pounds green beans, halved
1   cup chopped toasted walnuts
1   cup diced red onions
1   cup crumbled feta cheese

- Place beans in a large saucepan of boiling water and cook for 4 minutes. Drain immediately and rinse under cold water until cool. Pat dry and chill.
- Combine all ingredients for dressing and blend well.
- To serve, arrange the beans on a platter. Sprinkle with nuts, onions and cheese. Just before serving, add the dressing and toss.

Mint Dressing

¾   cup olive oil
¼   cup chopped fresh mint leaves
¼   cup white wine vinegar
¾   teaspoon salt or to taste
½   teaspoon minced garlic
¼   teaspoon pepper
½   tablespoon minced fresh basil leaves

POTATO SALAD WITH SUN-DRIED TOMATOES

Serves 6

6 cups thinly sliced potatoes, about 6 to 8 potatoes
½ cup olive oil (use some from the marinated tomatoes)
¼ cup white wine vinegar
½ cup sliced green onions, including green tops
1 red pepper, seeded and diced
1 green pepper, seeded and diced
1 cup chopped fresh parsley
⅔ cup slivered sun-dried tomatoes marinated in oil
salt and black pepper to taste

- Cook potatoes in boiling salted water until just tender, about 5 minutes. Drain.
- In a large salad bowl, combine potatoes with oil and vinegar. Let cool to room temperature.
- When potatoes are cool, add remaining ingredients and season with salt and pepper. Let stand for at least 30 minutes to allow the flavors to blend.

For those who love potato salad, but not the calories.

COUSCOUS SALAD

Serves 16

6 cups chicken stock
½ teaspoon ground ginger
½ teaspoon saffron
9 tablespoons olive oil, divided
3 cups couscous
¾ cup currants
¾ cup pitted and chopped dates
2¼ cups finely diced celery
1½ cups finely diced carrots
1 cup minced green onions
½ cup minced fresh parsley
2 tablespoons freshly squeezed lemon juice
¾ teaspoon salt or to taste
½ teaspoon cinnamon
¾ cup walnuts

- In a saucepan, bring stock, ginger, saffron, and 6 tablespoons oil to a boil. Add couscous and boil until the liquid begins to be absorbed.
- Remove from heat; mix in currants and dates. Cover and let stand for 15 minutes. Add celery, carrots and green onions. Mix well.
- In a small bowl, combine parsley, lemon juice, salt, cinnamon and remaining oil. Toss well with couscous, breaking up clumps. Cover and refrigerate overnight.
- Bring to room temperature. Taste, adjust seasonings and sprinkle with walnuts.

WILD RICE SALAD

Serves 10 to 12

½ pound fresh mushrooms, thinly sliced
  juice of 1 large lemon
1½ cups wild rice, cooked
1 red bell pepper, chopped
6 green onions, chopped
2 cups frozen tiny peas, thawed and drained

Dressing

2 garlic cloves, minced
2 teaspoons Dijon mustard
½ teaspoon salt
½ teaspoon pepper
¼ cup tarragon wine vinegar
⅓ cup canola oil
½ teaspoon dried tarragon or 2 teaspoons chopped
  fresh
¼ teaspoon sugar

- Combine mushrooms and lemon juice; marinate for several hours.
- Combine marinated mushrooms and juice with rice, red pepper and onions.
- Blend together all ingredients for dressing.
- Toss dressing with salad just before serving. Add peas at last minute and serve at room temperature.

DEVILED LENTIL SALAD

Serves 6 to 8

1   cup lentils
2   cups sliced mushrooms
⅓   cup chopped green onion
¼   cup chopped fresh parsley
1   small green pepper, chopped
1   small tomato, seeded and chopped
1   garlic clove, minced

Dressing

2   tablespoons salad oil
2   tablespoons olive oil
½   teaspoon salt
2½ tablespoons red wine vinegar
1   tablespoon Dijon mustard
1   teaspoon dried cilantro
½   teaspoon oregano
1   teaspoon Worcestershire sauce
3   drops hot red pepper sauce or to taste
    lettuce

- Boil lentils in 1 quart salted water until tender; drain.
- Combine lentils with mushrooms, green onions, parsley, green pepper, tomato and garlic.
- Combine all ingredients for dressing and blend well.
- Pour dressing over salad, mix and chill for at least 3 hours, stirring once or twice. Spoon over crisp lettuce.

CONFETTI SALAD

3   *cups shredded red cabbage*

1   *apple, cored and sliced*

½   *cup dried currants*

¼   *cup cooked whole-kernel corn, drained*

½   *cup green grapes*

2   *celery stalks, sliced*

⅔   *cup balsamic herb dressing*

Balsamic Herb Dressing

¼   *cup balsamic vinegar*

¼   *cup canola oil*

¼   *teaspoon onion powder*

¼   *teaspoon fine herbs*

¼   *teaspoon freshly ground black pepper*

⅛   *teaspoon dill weed*

¼   *teaspoon fennel seed*

- In a salad bowl mix cabbage, apple, currants, corn, grapes and celery.
- Blend all ingredients for balsamic herb dressing. Measure out ⅔ cup and pour over salad; toss to coat.

SAVOY CABBAGE SLAW WITH PEPPERS

Serves 6 to 8

1   small Savoy (curly) cabbage, about 1½ pounds,
    thinly shredded
½   cup slivered red bell pepper
½   cup slivered green pepper
½   cup chopped fresh parsley
½   cup thinly sliced green onions
2   tablespoons sugar
1½ teaspoons salt
½   teaspoon celery seed
½   cup white vinegar
⅓   cup salad oil

- In a large bowl combine cabbage, bell peppers, parsley and onions.
- In a large jar, shake together sugar, salt, celery seed, vinegar and oil until sugar dissolves.
- Pour dressing over cabbage mixture; mix lightly. Cover and refrigerate 30 minutes to 3 hours.

Unlike their leafy green salad cousins, cabbage salads can be made ahead. Refrigerating them for an hour or more enables flavors to blend and does not make the cabbage less crisp.

SPINACH SALAD WITH HOT VINAIGRETTE

Serves 6

8   garlic cloves, peeled
1   cup virgin olive oil
⅓   cup balsamic vinegar
1   tablespoon brown sugar
    salt and pepper to taste
6   cups washed and dried torn spinach
½   cup grated Parmesan cheese
2   ounces prosciutto, sliced very thin and torn into
    bite-size pieces
1   red bell pepper, sliced thin (optional)
1   red onion, sliced thin (optional)

- Cook garlic cloves in oil on medium heat until soft. Remove garlic from pan and chop.
- Add vinegar to oil and simmer 2 minutes; add brown sugar, salt, pepper and chopped garlic.
- Place spinach in large bowl; pour hot dressing over greens; top with cheese and pepper and onion if desired. Serve immediately.

SPINACH SALAD

- 1 bunch spinach
- 1 diced green apple
- ⅓ cup dry roasted Spanish peanuts
- ¼ cup golden raisins
- 5 green onions, thinly sliced
- 1 tablespoon sesame seed, toasted

Dressing

- 2 tablespoons white vinegar
- 1 tablespoon dry vermouth
- 2 tablespoons Dijon mustard
- 1 teaspoon soy sauce
- ½ teaspoon curry powder
- ½ teaspoon sugar
- ¼ teaspoon freshly ground pepper
- ⅓ cup salad oil

- Wash and dry spinach; tear into bite-size pieces.
- Combine all ingredients for dressing; mix well.
- Pour dressing in large bowl; top with spinach; DO NOT TOSS.
- Cover with plastic wrap and refrigerate. Toss just before serving.

CRANBERRY MOLD

- 1 3-ounce package raspberry jello
- 1 3-ounce package strawberry jello
- 3 cups boiling water
- 1 12-ounce can whole cranberry sauce
- 1 cup crushed pineapple with juice
- ½ to ¾ cup chopped pecans
- 3 tablespoons orange zest
- 1 orange, peeled and chopped

- Prepare gelatin mixtures in boiling water.
- Add cranberry sauce; stir until smooth. Add remaining ingredients.
- Pour into a 2-quart mold and chill until firm.

SPICED PEACH MOLD

Serves 10 to 12

 2   *3-ounce packages lemon jello*
 1   *tablespoon unflavored gelatin*
2½   *cups boiling water*
 1   *13-ounce can spiced peaches, drained, reserve*
     liquid
 ½   *cup lemon juice*
 1   *cup chopped walnuts*
 1   *cup chopped celery*
 2   *cups sour cream or yogurt*
     lettuce

- Prepare gelatin mixtures with boiling water.
- Add enough water to peach liquid to make 1½ cups. Add to gelatin mixture along with lemon juice.
- Cut peaches in ½-inch pieces; add to gelatin mixture with walnuts and celery. Blend in sour cream or yogurt.
- Pour into 9x12-inch pan or mold and chill until firm.
- Unmold and serve on a bed of lettuce.

LIME MINT FRUIT DRESSING

Makes ⅔ Cup

 ½   *cup Amaretto*
 ¼   *cup honey*
 2   *tablespoon lime juice*
4 to 6   *mint leaves, finely chopped*

- Mix all ingredients and pour over your favorite combination of fruit.
- Refrigerate about 2 hours.

FRUIT SALAD DRESSING

Makes 1⅔ Cups

1   teaspoon salt
1   teaspoon paprika
1   teaspoon dry mustard
1   teaspoon celery seed
1   teaspoon pepper
¼   cup lemon juice
¾   cup oil
⅓   cup honey

❧ Put all ingredients in a jar with a tight fitting cover. Shake hard and use as needed.

CREAMY CANTALOUPE DRESSING

Makes 2½ Cups

       juice of ½ lemon
1   envelope gelatin
½   cup apricot nectar, heated
⅓   cup sugar
1   cup diced cantaloupe
1   cup half and half or condensed skim milk
2   tablespoons rum

❧ Put lemon juice in blender and sprinkle in gelatin. Add hot nectar and blend for 1 minute.

❧ Add sugar and blend. While blender is still running, remove cover and add cantaloupe and cream or milk.

❧ Refrigerate until ready to serve.

❧ At serving time, stir in rum and pour sauce over fresh fruit compote.

Outstanding on fresh fruit!

DRESSING "A LA PALAZZO PIO"

Makes 1½ Cups

¼ cup Italian balsamic vinegar, scant
¾ cup extra virgin olive oil
¼ cup vermouth or gin
1 tablespoon capers

🍃 Mix all ingredients together. Serve over tender young lettuce leaves.

Quick, easy and good. What more could you ask for!

WALNUT OIL DRESSING

Makes ⅔ Cup

2 tablespoons tarragon wine vinegar
1 teaspoon lemon juice
2 teaspoons Dijon mustard
    salt and white pepper to taste
3 tablespoons walnut oil
⅓ cup salad oil

🍃 In a medium bowl, mix vinegar, lemon juice, mustard, salt and pepper.
🍃 Using a whisk or fork, gradually beat in oil until well blended and thickened.

Great with green salads.

LOW CAL DRESSING

Makes ½ Cup

½ cup rice wine vinegar
½ teaspoon fresh grated ginger
1 tablespoon chopped fresh parsley
1 tablespoon soy sauce

🍃 Combine ingredients in container with tight fitting lid. Shake well.

MEATS

FILET MIGNON WITH RED WINE SAUCE

Serves 6

3   cups dry red wine

3   tablespoons cognac

3   shallots, chopped

1   tablespoon chopped fresh thyme or 1 teaspoon
dried

6   6-ounce filet mignon steaks

4   cups beef stock

4   tablespoons olive oil
salt and pepper to taste

2½ tablespoons chilled unsalted butter, cut into pieces

❧ Whisk first 4 ingredients in large bowl. Divide steaks between 2 glass baking dishes. Pour marinade over. Cover and refrigerate overnight.

❧ Remove steaks from marinade and pat dry. Transfer marinade to heavy large saucepan. Boil until reduced to 1 cup, about 20 minutes. Add stock and boil about 20 minutes to reduce to 1¼ cups; set aside. (Cover and refrigerate steaks and sauce separately up to four hours. Bring steaks to room temperature.)

❧ Divide oil between 2 heavy large skillets; place over high heat. Season steaks with salt and pepper. Add 3 steaks to each skillet and brown on both sides. Reduce heat to medium-high and cook to desired doneness, about 4 minutes per side for medium rare. Transfer steaks to plates. Keep warm.

❧ Add half of sauce to each skillet and bring to boil. Combine sauce in 1 skillet and bring to simmer. Add butter and whisk until melted. Spoon sauce over steaks and serve.

TENDERLOIN OF BEEF WITH MUSTARD AND HORSERADISH SAUCE

Serves 6

Sauce

- *1   cup sour cream*
- *3   tablespoons Dijon mustard*
- *2   tablespoons prepared horseradish*

Tenderloin

- *2   teaspoons whole black peppercorns*
- *2   teaspoons whole white peppercorns*
- *2   teaspoons whole green peppercorns*
- *2   teaspoons coarse salt*
- *3   tablespoons Dijon mustard*
- *2   tablespoons butter or margarine, at room temperature*
- *1   cup loosely packed chopped fresh Italian parsley*
- *2   pounds tenderloin of beef, trimmed*
  parsley sprigs for garnish

Sauce

- Whisk all ingredients in small bowl. Cover and refrigerate until ready to serve. Can be prepared a day ahead.

Tenderloin

- Coarsely grind all peppercorns; transfer to bowl. Mix in salt. Whisk mustard, butter and parsley in medium bowl to blend. Rub over tenderloin. Roll in peppercorn mixture, coating completely.
- Place tenderloin on rack set in shallow baking pan. Roast at 450 degrees until meat thermometer inserted into center registers 130 degrees for rare, about 35 minutes. Cook longer for more well done meat. Transfer to platter. Let stand 10 minutes. Cut into slices and arrange on platter. Surround with parsley. Serve with sauce.

COLD FILLET OF BEEF, JAPONAIS

Serves 8 to 10

1   *large fillet of beef, 5 to 6 pounds, trimmed of all fat*
⅓   *cup soy sauce*
½   *cup olive oil or peanut oil*
1   *cup sherry*
6   *chopped garlic cloves*
1   *teaspoon hot pepper sauce*
      dash freshly ground pepper
      watercress and cherry tomatoes for garnish

- Marinate the fillet in the rest of the ingredients, except watercress and tomatoes, for 24 hours, turning several times. Remove and dry.
- Rub with additional oil, and roast on a broiling rack at 475 degrees for 25 minutes for very rare, 28 to 30 minutes for rare. Baste with marinade 3 or 4 times during the roasting. Allow to cool to room temperature. If possible, do not refrigerate.
- Arrange on a platter with watercress and cherry tomatoes.

ENTRECÔTE MARCHAND DE VIN, "BEEF IN WINE SAUCE"

Serves 4

4   *rib or club steaks, each 1-inch thick*
8   *tablespoons butter or margarine, divided*
½   *cup dry red wine*
3   *tablespoons minced shallots (or white portions of green onions)*
¼   *teaspoon thyme*
      salt and pepper to taste
      minced parsley

- Sauté steaks in 2 tablespoons butter or margarine in a large iron skillet turning once so that both sides are seared and meat is medium rare (or as you like it). Allow 6 to 7 minutes per side for rare. Remove steaks from pan and keep warm.
- Pour fat from pan and add wine, shallots, thyme, salt and pepper. Simmer until wine has almost evaporated and becomes a thick syrup.
- Remove pan from heat and stir in remaining butter or margarine, a spoonful at a time, until sauce is smooth and thick. Adjust seasonings, stir in parsley and spoon over steaks.

ROAST BEEF SANDWICHES WITH CAPER VINAIGRETTE   *Serves 4*

3   *tablespoons fresh lemon juice*
2   *teaspoons country-style Dijon mustard*
¼   *cup olive oil*
    freshly ground pepper to taste
2   *tablespoons capers, drained*
8   *slices French bread*
1   *pound thinly sliced deli roast beef*

- Whisk together the lemon juice and mustard. Slowly add the olive oil and whisk until smooth. Stir in pepper and capers.
- Toast bread under a hot broiler.
- To serve, lay slices of roast beef over 4 slices of bread, drizzle with the vinaigrette and top with remaining slices of bread.

For one of those days when the desire to pamper is strong but time is short.

BEEF CURRY WITH FRUIT   *Serves 6*

1½ *pounds lean trimmed chuck roast cut into 1-inch cubes*
1   *10½-ounce can beef broth, divided*
2   *tablespoons lemon juice*
1   *tablespoon light soy sauce*
4   *tablespoons raisins or currants*
    salt and pepper to taste
1   *tablespoon curry powder*
2   *onions, thinly sliced*
3   *tablespoons flour*
2   *red apples, unpeeled and diced*
3   *tablespoons dry roasted peanuts or cashews*

- Brown beef in skillet. Discard any fat. Stir in 1 cup of broth. Add lemon juice, soy sauce, raisins, seasonings and onions. Cover and simmer 1 to 1½ hours.
- Stir flour into remaining broth and add mixture to pan, stirring until mixture is thick.
- Add apples and nuts just before serving or serve on side as condiments.

Just about any kinds of fruits can be used. Be creative!

SHAMROCK BEEF

Serves 8

1   *corned beef brisket, 2 to 4 pounds*
    water
4   *tablespoons firmly packed brown sugar*
2   *tablespoons prepared mustard*
⅛   *teaspoon ground cloves*
8   *red potatoes*
8   *peeled carrots*
2   *turnips, peeled and cut in quarters*
1   *cabbage, cut in wedges*
    parsley for garnish

❦ Place corned beef, with enough water to cover, in a large Dutch oven. Cover and simmer about 1 hour for each pound of meat.

❦ Mix sugar, mustard and cloves. Remove meat, spread top with mustard mixture. Bake at 350 degrees for 20 minutes.

❦ Meanwhile, pour off half of cooking liquid. Add potatoes, carrots and turnips. Cover and cook 10 to 15 minutes. Add cabbage and cook 10 more minutes until vegetables are tender.

❦ To serve meat, cut slices across grain. Garnish with parsley.

BEEF IN OYSTER SAUCE

Serves 2

2   *tablespoons bottled oyster sauce*
1   *tablespoon dry sherry*
½   *teaspoon sugar*
1   *teaspoon cornstarch*
2   *tablespoons vegetable oil*
12 *ounces sirloin steak, cut into thin bite-size pieces*
4   *green onions, cut into 1½-inch pieces*
4   *mushrooms, sliced*
5   *water chestnuts, sliced*

❦ Mix oyster sauce, sherry, sugar and cornstarch.

❦ Heat oil in wok or skillet. Add beef and stir until brown; add vegetables and mix well. Stir in sauce mixture. Remove as soon as sauce is clear and thickened.

❦ Serve at once with steamed rice.

A variety of vegetables can be used such as pea pods, asparagus, green beans and/or broccoli.

GREEN CHILE BEEF STEW

Serves 4 to 6

2   tablespoons salad oil
2   pounds beef stew meat (brisket, if available)
2   large onions, thinly sliced
1   4-ounce can chopped green chilies
1   16-ounce can Italian style tomatoes, coarsely
    chopped
1   cup regular strength chicken broth
    salt to taste
1   avocado, diced
    sour cream
2   limes, cut into wedges

&» Heat oil in a 5-quart kettle over medium heat. Add meat and cook until browned. Lift out and put aside in bowl.

&» Add onions to pan and cook, stirring, until soft. Return meat and juices to pan, add chilies, tomatoes and their liquid, and broth. Bring to a boil; cover, reduce heat, and simmer until meat is tender (about 2½ hours). Season with salt.

&» Spoon stew into individual bowls; serve with avocado and sour cream, and lime wedges to squeeze over top.

GREEK-STYLE BEEF STEW

Serves 4 to 6

2   pounds beef chuck, cut into 2-inch pieces
     all purpose flour for dredging
½   cup olive oil
2½   pounds small white onions, blanched in boiling
     water for 1 minute, drained, and peeled leaving
     the root ends intact
1   8-ounce can tomato sauce
½   cup red wine vinegar
5   garlic cloves
1   tablespoon pickling spice, tied in a cheesecloth bag
     (optional)

&» Dredge beef in flour, shaking off the excess. In a large kettle heat oil over moderately high heat until it is hot, but not smoking. Add beef and brown in batches; transfer meat with a slotted spoon to a bowl.

&» To fat in kettle add onions, tomato sauce, vinegar, garlic, browned beef and pickling spice. Bring liquid to a boil; cover and simmer for 2½ to 3 hours, stirring occasionally.

KOREAN BEEF STRIPS

Serves 4

3   pounds top round steak or beef chuck roast

½   cup soy sauce

½   cup minced green onions

2   cloves garlic, minced

4   teaspoons sesame seeds

2   teaspoons sugar

1   teaspoon finely minced fresh ginger or ½ teaspoon
ground

⅓   cup sesame oil

- For easy slicing, partially freeze meat. Then cut into ¼ inch slices.
- Stir together remaining ingredients in a large bowl. Add beef strips and marinate 3 to 6 hours in refrigerator.
- To barbecue, skewer beef and cook all at once.
- To broil, spread beef out on foil-covered baking sheet.

"SAVOY" MEAT LOAF

Serves 6

½   pound ground beef

½   pound ground pork

½   pound ground veal

1½   cups chopped fresh spinach

¾   cup fresh white bread crumbs

½   cup chopped pistachios

2   large garlic cloves, chopped

1   teaspoon chopped fresh thyme or ¼ teaspoon dried

½   teaspoon fresh rosemary or ⅛ teaspoon dried

½   teaspoon ground nutmeg

2   large eggs

2   tablespoons Dijon mustard

¼   teaspoon hot pepper sauce
salt and pepper to taste

3 to 4   bacon slices

- Combine beef, pork, veal, spinach, bread crumbs, pistachios, garlic, thyme, rosemary and nutmeg in bowl.
- Mix eggs, mustard and hot pepper sauce in small bowl. Add to meat and mix. Season with salt and pepper.
- Line a 9x5-inch glass loaf dish with bacon slices. Spread meat mixture into dish. Smooth top. (Can be prepared 4 hours ahead. Cover and refrigerate.)
- Place dish in larger deep baking pan. Add enough water to come half way up loaf pan. Bake at 400 degrees until loaf is firm and brown and sides pull away from dish, about 55 minutes. Invert onto platter. Remove bacon. Slice and serve.

BASIL ROASTED PORK

Serves 4

3   tablespoons olive oil
2   tablespoons chopped fresh basil
2   large garlic cloves, minced
1   tablespoon olive oil
4   8-ounce pork tenderloin pieces (or 1 boneless pork loin)
    salt and pepper to taste

❧ Combine first three ingredients. Coat pork with basil mixture. Season generously with pepper and place in pan or plastic bag. Refrigerate for at least 4 hours.

❧ Heat oil in large heavy oven proof skillet over medium-high heat. Season pork with salt if desired. Brown in skillet about 8 to 10 minutes. Transfer to oven and roast at 350 degrees for about 20 minutes or until centers register 150 degrees. Rest 10 minutes before slicing.

Great with Corn Risotto in our "Grains, Pasta and Sides" section!

PORK À L'ORANGE

Serves 6

1   cup orange juice
⅓   cup soy sauce
¼   cup olive oil
2   tablespoons chopped fresh rosemary or 2 teaspoons dried, crumbled
3   cloves garlic, pressed
2   12-ounce pork tenderloins (or boneless pork loin)
    freshly ground black pepper

❧ Combine first five ingredients in non-metallic baking dish. Add pork and marinate in refrigerator at least 1 hour or overnight.

❧ Drain pork; reserve marinade. Place pork on baking sheet or pan. Season generously with pepper. Roast 20 minutes for tenderloins, about 1 hour for loin, or until cooked through.

❧ Heat reserved marinade to boiling. Slice pork tenderloins and pass marinade separately as a sauce.

TENDERLOIN AU SHERRY

Serves 6

1   2-pound pork tenderloin
    salt and pepper to taste
1   tablespoon vegetable oil
½   cup water
½   pound fresh mushrooms, sliced
1   tablespoon butter or margarine
    flour
4   tablespoons sherry

- Salt and pepper tenderloin and brown on all sides in hot oil in skillet. Add water, cover and simmer until done, about 30 minutes. Add more water as needed.
- Sauté mushrooms in butter or margarine.
- Remove tenderloin from skillet, keep warm. Use remaining juices and flour to make a gravy.
- Add sherry to taste, then mushrooms. Pour over meat and serve.

CAJUN PORK ROAST

Serves 6

2   pounds boneless loin pork roast (or 1 rolled and tied double-loin roast)
3   tablespoons paprika
½   teaspoon cayenne pepper
1   tablespoon garlic powder
2   teaspoons oregano
2   teaspoons thyme
½   teaspoon salt
½   teaspoon white pepper
½   teaspoon cumin
¼   teaspoon nutmeg

- Combine all seasonings and rub well over all surfaces of the roast. Place roast in shallow pan and roast in 350 degree oven for about 1 hour, or until internal temperature is 155 to 160 degrees. Remove from oven; let rest 5 to 10 minutes before slicing.

PORK MEDALLIONS WITH CURRANTS

Serves 4 to 6

⅓ cup currants

½ cup Scotch whiskey or sherry

2 pork tenderloins, about ¾ to 1 pound each, or 2 pounds pork chops, visible fat removed

salt and white pepper to taste

2 tablespoons unsalted butter

½ cup chicken stock

3 tablespoons Dijon mustard

3 tablespoons brown sugar

1 teaspoon dried thyme

- Combine currants and Scotch or sherry in small bowl. Set aside.

- Cut the tenderloins in ¾-inch fillets, reserving pointed ends for another use. Season with salt and white pepper.

- Heat butter in a heavy-bottomed skillet over medium-high heat. Brown the fillets quickly for about 1 minute on each side. Lower the heat and cook an additional 5 to 6 minutes on each side. Remove the fillets and keep warm. Pour off any accumulated fat in the pan.

- Drain the currants, reserving the liquid. Add liquid to the skillet, stirring to scrape up drippings. Stir in the stock, mustard, sugar and thyme.

- Whisk until smooth. Bring mixture to a boil and thicken slightly. Reduce heat and add currants and fillets. Cover pan and heat fillets in sauce for about 3 minutes. Place the fillets on warm plates, spooning sauce over them.

Variation: Try chicken breasts or thighs with sherry.

CHUTNEY CHOPS

2   *lean thick-cut pork chops*
1   *apple, cored and sliced in thick rings*
1   *medium yellow or white onion, thickly sliced*
1   *teaspoon galangal powder*
⅓   *cup chutney, chopped if chunky*
¼   *cup red wine*

- Rinse chops, pat dry.
- Layer apple rings and onions in a 2-quart baking dish. Add chops, sprinkle with galangal powder, and spread chutney over them.
- Pour on red wine, cover and bake at 350 degrees for 1 hour. Serve hot.

This one is so simple, it's almost cheating! And it's so good. The chutney gives it more complexity than it deserves. Galangal is a milder relative of ginger; substitute ¼ teaspoon powdered ginger if galangal is unavailable.

PORK MEDALLIONS WITH SORREL SAUCE

Serves 2

2   lean pork medallions

1   teaspoon cracked peppercorns

2   teaspoons olive oil

2   shallots, thinly sliced

2   tablespoons fresh minced mint

1   bunch fresh sorrel, trimmed and shredded; reserve
    a few leaves for garnish

¼   cup dry white wine

- Rinse pork, pat dry and press cracked peppercorns into both sides of medallions.

- Heat oil in heavy skillet, add pork and shallots and brown, cooking for 6 to 8 minutes on each side; transfer to warm plates and hold in warm oven.

- Add mint and sorrel to pan drippings, stir and cook for 1 to 2 minutes until limp. Add wine, stir and cook for 2 to 3 minutes. Pulse in blender or food processor a few seconds until smooth and frothy. Pour over warm pork and serve at once. Garnish with sorrel leaves.

Serve this in spring and fall when fresh sorrel is found in the market. The sauce is also wonderful with halibut or swordfish as well as broiled chicken.

PORK CHOPS IN SAKE MARINADE

Serves 4

2   *cups sake or dry white wine*

½   *cup thinly sliced green onions*

¼   *cup finely chopped fresh ginger*

2   *tablespoons soy sauce*

2   *cloves garlic, minced*

4   *pork chops (1½-inches thick, about 2 pounds total), fat removed*

2   *tablespoons Oriental sesame oil or salad oil*

- In a 9x13-inch pan mix sake, onion, ginger, soy sauce and garlic. Place chops in marinade; cover and refrigerate 2 hours or as long as overnight. Turn chops occasionally.

- Pour oil into 10 to 12-inch skillet over medium-high heat. Remove chops from marinade and place in pan, reserving marinade. Cook and turn until well browned on both sides, about 10 minutes.

- Add marinade to pan; bring to boil. Cover and simmer until chops are tender when pierced, about 50 minutes. Turn chops midway through cooking period.

- Transfer chops to platter; keep warm. Skim fat from pan juices and bring juices to a boil. Cook, uncovered, until reduced to ⅔ cup. Spoon over chops and serve.

Put fresh ginger in thin slices through your garlic press.

SWEET AND SOUR RIBS

Serves 4 to 6

2 pounds meaty pork ribs
2 tablespoons vegetable oil
¾ cup water
¼ cup brown sugar
2 tablespoons cornstarch
1 teaspoon salt
1 cup pineapple juice
⅓ cup vinegar
1 tablespoon soy sauce
½ cup green pepper strips
¼ cup thinly sliced onions
2½ cups pineapple chunks, drained

❧ Brown ribs in hot oil. Add water. Cover and cook slowly until tender (1½ to 2 hours) adding more water if necessary. Drain off fat.

❧ Combine sugar and cornstarch. Add salt, pineapple juice, vinegar and soy sauce. Cook over low heat until thick, stirring constantly. Pour sauce over hot ribs and let stand 10 minutes.

❧ Add green pepper, onion and pineapple chunks. Cook 5 minutes.

GRILLED PORK AND RED PEPPER SANDWICHES

Serves 6

2 teaspoons olive oil
2 garlic cloves, minced
  juice and grated rind of 1 orange, lemon or lime
1 teaspoon fresh lemon thyme or thyme
  few leaves fresh sage, chopped, or ¼ teaspoon dried sage, crumbled
  salt and pepper to taste
3 to 4 pound pork loin roast cut into strips at least ¾-inch thick and 4 to 5-inches long
3 red, green or yellow bell peppers, cut lengthwise into 1-inch strips

❧ Combine olive oil, garlic, juice and rind, thyme, sage and salt and pepper for marinade. Add pork and peppers and set aside until ready to cook.

❧ When coals are ready, thread pork on bamboo skewers. Place over coals and cook for 3 to 4 minutes on each side, brushing with more marinade before turning. Place pepper strips at outer edges of grill, turn after 5 to 6 minutes.

These lovely and quickly cooked morsels may be eaten right off the stick like kebabs, or dressed up a bit, slathered with a savory herb and yogurt sauce and wrapped into warm flour tortillas, pitas or chewy tannour breads for sandwiches. Great picnic food!

VEAL WITH GLAZED GREEN ONIONS

Serves 6

6   green onions thinly sliced, green and white parts
    separated
⅓   cup plus 2 tablespoons clarified butter for sautéing
¼   cup dry white wine
½   cup heavy cream
12 tablespoons butter, divided
    salt and freshly ground white pepper to taste
6   6-ounce fillets or sirloin chops of veal
7   green onions (green portion only), thinly sliced
1   tablespoon sugar

- Blanch the white portion of the 6 green onions in boiling salted water for 3 to 5 minutes. Refresh in ice water, drain and set aside.

- Sauce: Heat 2 tablespoons clarified butter and sauté the green portion of the 6 green onions over medium-high heat for 3 to 4 minutes. Add the white wine and boil for 5 minutes. Puree in a food processor and return to the skillet. Add the heavy cream and reduce by half. Swirl in 10 tablespoons of the butter. Season to taste, set aside and keep warm.

- Heat ⅓ cup clarified butter in another oven proof skillet and quickly sauté the veal over medium-high heat on both sides until golden. Place the skillet in a 400 degree oven for about 6 minutes or until veal is cooked through. Remove to covered plate and keep warm.

- To the same pan, add the remaining 2 tablespoons butter and allow to brown slightly. Sauté the blanched green onions and all remaining green onions. Add the sugar and heat through until the green onions are glazed.

- Carve the veal diagonally from the top corner on 1 side to the bottom corner opposite, 2 triangles per fillet. Pour the scallion sauce on warmed plates or platter, arrange veal slices and garnish with glazed green onions.

VEAL ROAST POMMERY

  1 *veal roast, approximately 3 pounds (rolled boned leg, loin or rump)*
     Herbes de Provence (available on spice shelves, contains marjoram, thyme, summer savory, basil, rosemary, sage, fennel and lavender)
     salt and cracked pepper to taste
     grated zest and juice of 1 lemon
 ¼ *cup butter, melted*
  1 *cup white wine*
     Pommery grain mustard or other dark coarse grained mustard
  2 *tablespoons flour*
  1 *tablespoon butter*

Herb Crumbs

  1 *cup fresh bread crumbs*
  1 *teaspoon minced garlic*
 ¼ *cup chopped parsley*
  6 *tablespoons butter, melted*

* Season roast liberally with Herbes de Provence, salt, pepper, lemon zest and lemon juice. In roasting pan, heat butter and brown veal well on all sides.

* Roast in 375 degree oven for 30 minutes. Add wine to pan and baste veal frequently until cooked, approximately 15 to 30 minutes more. Juices should run slightly pink when a skewer is inserted. Remove from pan and strain off juices.

* Combine all ingredients for Herb Crumbs and mix well. Cover veal with mustard and pat crumbs evenly on surface of the roast. Return the roast to the pan and place in a 450 degree oven to glaze, approximately 10 minutes, or until the crust is crisp and golden.

* Pour the pan juices into a heavy saucepan, add ¼ cup white wine or water and thicken slightly with a beurre manie (flour mixed with softened butter). Spoon some of the sauce over the veal slices and serve the rest of the sauce separately.

TUNA SAUCE FOR VEAL

  1 *can water-packed tuna*
     juice of 1 small lemon
  1 *teaspoon capers*
  1 *garlic clove, minced or ¼ teaspoon garlic puree*
 ¼ *cup extra virgin olive oil*

* Blend all ingredients except olive oil in processor or blender. Add oil gradually until desired consistency.

This is used by Italian cooks to coat a small roast of veal in final minutes of cooking, or slices of cold veal that have been poached in chicken stock. This sauce is also good on cold turkey breast or on pita bread triangles!

VEAL MARENGO

8 tablespoons butter or margarine, divided
2 tablespoons vegetable oil
2 pounds boneless veal cut into 1½-inch cubes
1 small onion, finely chopped
   salt and freshly ground pepper to taste
2 tablespoons flour
1 cup dry white wine
1 cup chicken stock
2 tomatoes, peeled, seeded and chopped
1 cup canned Italian tomatoes, drained, seeded and chopped
1 garlic clove, minced
½ teaspoon dried thyme
½ pound fresh mushrooms, halved
12 small white onions
1 tablespoon sugar
10 pimiento-stuffed green olives, sliced (optional)

Bouquet Garni

4 sprigs parsley
1 celery stalk with leaves
1 bay leaf

- In a large flameproof casserole, heat 2 tablespoons of the butter or margarine and the oil over moderately high heat. Quickly brown the veal, patted dry, a few pieces at a time. Remove veal and reserve juices.

- Add another 2 tablespoons of butter to the casserole and sauté the onion until light brown. Sprinkle with salt, pepper and flour and cook 3 minutes to allow the flour to color lightly.

- Return the veal to the casserole. Add the wine, stock, fresh and canned tomatoes, garlic, bouquet garni and thyme. Bring to a boil, cover and bake at 325 degrees for 30 minutes.

- Meanwhile, sauté the mushrooms in 2 tablespoons of butter or margarine over moderately high heat for 3 to 4 minutes and set aside. In the same skillet, heat the remaining 2 tablespoons of butter or margarine, add the white onions, sprinkle them with sugar and sauté until golden brown, about 10 minutes.

- Add mushrooms and white onions to the stew and bake until the veal is tender, about 40 minutes more.

- To serve, taste for seasoning, remove bouquet garni and add the sliced green olives, if desired. While not part of a traditional marengo, the olives are a piquant addition.

VEAL PAPRIKA

2 *pounds boneless veal stew meat, cut in 1½-inch cubes*
2 *tablespoons butter or margarine*
2 *tablespoons oil*
1 *garlic clove, minced*
1 *medium onion, thinly sliced*
2 *tablespoons flour*
1½ *teaspoons salt*
   chicken stock or water
1 *cup sour cream*
1 *tablespoon paprika*

- Brown veal in hot butter and oil. Add garlic and onions and cook until softened.
- Mix flour and salt and sprinkle over meat. Mix well.
- Add stock or water to barely cover meat. Cover and cook slowly, 1 hour, or until veal is tender, adding more liquid as necessary.
- Stir in sour cream and paprika. Heat, but do not boil.

VEAL PARMESAN

2 *pounds veal cutlets or scallops, ½-inch thick*
1½ *teaspoons salt*
¼ *teaspoon freshly ground black pepper*
1½ *teaspoons crumbled dried basil leaves*
½ *cup grated Parmesan cheese*
1½ *cups fine, dry bread crumbs*
3 *eggs, beaten*
3 *tablespoons butter or margarine*
3 *tablespoons vegetable oil*
   lemon slices

- Flatten serving-size pieces of veal to ¼-inch thickness with a mallet. Mix salt, pepper and basil. Rub into both sides of meat.
- Blend cheese and bread crumbs. Roll meat in crumbs, dip in egg and roll in crumbs again. Let stand at least ½ hour so that crumbs will adhere.
- Heat butter and oil in skillet. Cook veal on both sides until brown and just cooked through, about 10 minutes each side. Garnish with fresh lemon slices.

BUTTERFLIED LEG OF LAMB

Serves 8 to 12

1   tablespoon plus 1 teaspoon olive oil

1   teaspoon soy sauce

1   tablespoon finely chopped fresh rosemary or
     tarragon or 1 teaspoon dried, divided

1   leg of lamb, 6 to 7 pounds, trimmed of fat, boned
     and butterflied

2   large garlic cloves, each cut into 12 slivers

3   tablespoons lemon juice

Sauce

1   large garlic clove, crushed and chopped

1   tablespoon lemon juice

¾   teaspoon fresh thyme or ¼ teaspoon dried

1   tablespoon finely chopped fresh parsley

- In a small bowl, combine 1 tablespoon of the olive oil with the soy sauce and 2 teaspoons of the fresh rosemary or tarragon or ¾ teaspoon of the dried. Rub the lamb all over with the mixture.

- With a small sharp knife, make 24 slits in the boned side of the lamb and insert a garlic sliver in each. Rub the lamb with the remaining olive oil and rosemary or tarragon and pour the lemon juice over all.

- Place the lamb, boned side down, on a broiler rack with its pan. Roast in a 400 degree oven for 25 minutes or until internal temperature reaches 130 degrees. Turn the oven to broil and place the lamb about five inches from the heat. Broil 2 to 3 minutes until it starts to brown. Transfer the lamb to a carving board and let rest for 10 minutes.

- For the sauce, stir the garlic, lemon juice and thyme into the pan juices; cover and keep warm.

- Carve the lamb and transfer the slices to a serving platter. Stir the parsley into the sauce and pour it over the lamb or pass separately.

INDONESIAN LAMB SAUTÉ

Serves 6

2　medium onions, finely chopped
1 to 2　garlic cloves, minced
¼　cup smooth peanut butter
2　tablespoons brown sugar
¼　teaspoon salt
¼　teaspoon crushed dried red pepper or to taste
¼　cup soy sauce
3　tablespoons lemon juice
2　pounds boned leg of lamb, cut into 1-inch cubes

- Combine all ingredients except lamb in a bowl; mix well. Add lamb and marinate in the refrigerator overnight.
- Skewer meat; reserve marinade. Grill over coals or broil 3 inches from the source of the heat for ten minutes on each side, brushing occasionally with the marinade.

PERUVIAN SHOULDER CHOPS WITH GREEN ONIONS

Serves 4

3　tablespoons flour
1　teaspoon salt or to taste
¼　teaspoon pepper
½　teaspoon oregano
4　lamb shoulder chops, about ¾-inch thick
¼　cup vegetable oil
¼　cup chopped green onions
¼　cup coffee
¼　cup sour cream
¼　cup, about 1 ounce, grated Gruyere cheese

- Combine flour, salt and pepper, and oregano. Pound the flour mixture into the lamb.
- Heat the oil and brown lamb on both sides. Add green onions and sauté briefly. Arrange lamb and green onions in a greased shallow casserole.
- Combine coffee and sour cream and pour over the lamb. Top with cheese and bake at 350 degrees for 30 minutes.

LEBANESE BURGERS

1½   *pounds lean ground lamb*
½   *onion, finely chopped*
½   *cup chopped parsley*
1   *teaspoon salt*
1   *teaspoon cinnamon*
1   *teaspoon cumin*
1   *teaspoon paprika*
½   *teaspoon cayenne pepper*
2   *tablespoons cold water*

Yogurt Sauce

2   *cups plain yogurt*
1   *garlic clove, minced*
¼   *teaspoon salt*
½   *tablespoon dried mint or 1 tablespoon fresh mint*
1   *teaspoon cumin*
1   *tomato, diced and drained*
½   *cup diced cucumber, drained*

- Mix ingredients for yogurt sauce and set aside.
- Mix lamb with remaining ingredients. Shape into patties. Barbecue or broil.
- Spoon sauce over patties and serve in pita bread.

POULTRY

CHICKEN MARBELLA

4   *chickens, 2½ pounds each, quartered*
1   *whole head of garlic, peeled and finely puréed*
¼   *cup dried oregano*
     coarse salt and freshly ground black pepper to taste
½   *cup red wine vinegar*
¼   *cup olive oil*
1   *cup pitted prunes*
½   *cup pitted Spanish green olives, rinsed*
½   *cup capers with a bit of juice*
6   *bay leaves*
1   *cup brown sugar*
1   *cup white wine*
¼   *cup finely chopped Italian parsley or fresh cilantro*

- In a large bowl combine chicken quarters, garlic, oregano, pepper and coarse salt to taste, vinegar, olive oil, prunes, olives, capers with juice, and bay leaves. Cover and let marinate, refrigerated, overnight.

- Arrange chicken in a single layer in 2 large shallow baking pans and spoon marinade over evenly. Sprinkle chicken pieces with brown sugar and pour white wine around them. Bake at 350 degrees for 50 to 60 minutes, basting frequently with pan juices. Remove bay leaves.

- With a slotted spoon transfer chicken, prunes, olives and capers to a serving platter. Moisten with a few spoonfuls of pan juices and sprinkle generously with parsley or cilantro. Pass remaining pan juices at table.

To serve Chicken Marbella cold, cool to room temperature in cooking juices before transferring to a serving platter. If chicken has been covered and refrigerated, allow it to return to room temperature. This chicken dish keeps and even improves over several days in the refrigerator. It travels well and makes excellent picnic fare.

COLD POACHED CHICKEN BREASTS WITH RED PEPPER PURÉE

Serves 6

3   cups chicken broth or enough to cover chicken

3   whole skinless and boneless chicken breasts cut in half

2   red bell peppers, cut in halves

1   teaspoon olive oil

2   cloves garlic, minced

1   tablespoon chopped fresh basil or 1 teaspoon dried basil, crushed

2   tablespoons balsamic vinegar

¼   teaspoon salt or to taste
    freshly ground black pepper to taste

- In a medium-sized skillet bring chicken broth to a boil. Add chicken, cover and simmer 5 to 7 minutes. Remove from heat and let chicken remain in broth for 30 minutes.

- Remove chicken from broth and refrigerate until chilled. Reserve broth for another use.

- Place peppers on a broiler pan or foil and broil until skins blacken and blister. Remove from oven and cover with wet paper towels. When cool, remove the blackened skin and seeds.

- Heat olive oil over medium heat, add garlic and sauté until lightly browned. Purée the peppers in a food processor with the sautéed garlic, basil, vinegar, salt and pepper. Refrigerate for at least 1 hour to blend flavors.

- To serve, slice the chicken on the diagonal and top with purée. Garnish with basil leaves and serve the extra sauce on the side.

The purée can be added to light mayonnaise, yogurt or vinaigrette for a refreshing sauce.

CHICKEN BREASTS WITH WALNUT STUFFING

Serves 4

3 *cups toasted bread cubes*
6 *tablespoons butter or margarine, melted, divided*
⅓ *cup chopped onion*
½ *cup chopped celery*
2 *teaspoons parsley flakes*
¾ *cup chopped walnuts*
4 *small chicken breasts, boned*
   lemon juice
   salt and pepper to taste

- Mix together bread cubes, half the melted butter, onion, celery, parsley and walnuts; add enough water to moisten. Grease the center of 4 squares of heavy duty foil with butter or margarine and place on a cookie sheet. Mound stuffing on each oiled center.
- Brush both sides of the chicken breasts with lemon juice, then brush with the remaining butter. Sprinkle with salt and pepper.
- Place 1 chicken breast over each mound of stuffing. Fold the foil around the top of the chicken to make individual sealed packages.
- Bake 30 minutes at 350 degrees, then open each package and bake for an additional 10 minutes at 400 degrees. It is important at this stage to check the meat carefully so that it does not become overcooked.

In a hurry? Replace the toasted bread cubes with packaged stuffing mix. Need an easy, make-ahead recipe to prepare for a large dinner party? This is it!

ROSEMARY CHICKEN BREASTS

Serves 8

⅓ cup rosemary flavored olive oil (See note.)
¼ cup sherry vinegar
4 cloves of garlic, chopped
½ cup chopped fresh parsley
1 tablespoon chopped fresh rosemary or 1 teaspoon
   dried rosemary
8 boneless, skinless chicken breast halves
   salt and freshly ground pepper to taste
   Hungarian sweet paprika

๛ Combine the olive oil, sherry vinegar, garlic, parsley and rosemary in a non-metal container, large enough to hold the chicken breasts. Marinate 2 hours (not more) in the refrigerator.

๛ Arrange the chicken on a preheated grill or broiler pan. Sprinkle with salt, pepper and paprika. Grill or broil 4 minutes each side. Do not overcook. Serve hot or at room temperature.

Marinate a bit of rosemary in the olive oil a day or two before preparing this dish.

KASHMIR CHICKEN

Serves 4 to 6

6   boneless, skinless chicken breast halves
    flour, salt and pepper to dust
1   tablespoon butter or margarine (add more as
    needed)
1   onion, chopped
1   green pepper, chopped
1   teaspoon cumin
1   teaspoon caraway seeds
¼   teaspoon turmeric
    cayenne pepper to taste
1   tomato, diced

Sauce for Baking

½   teaspoon ground cloves
¼   teaspoon grated nutmeg
1   teaspoon crushed cardamom
1   cup yogurt or sour cream
4   tablespoons brown sugar

❧ Salt and pepper the chicken breasts and lightly coat with flour. Heat butter in skillet at medium heat and cook chicken in butter or margarine until golden brown. Remove from pan.

❧ Add to the pan the onion, green pepper, cumin, caraway seeds, turmeric, and cayenne. Cook on medium heat at least 10 minutes, stirring frequently. Return the chicken to the pan and add the diced tomato. Simmer about 20 minutes. Remove the chicken and put in an ovenproof dish.

❧ Stir the sauce ingredients into the pan with the onions, etc. Pour mixture over the chicken, bake at 325 degrees, uncovered, until bubbling and hot, about 20 minutes.

❧ Serve with a pilaf or an aromatic rice like Basmatic rice.

CHICKEN BREASTS WITH CRAB STUFFING

Serves 8

8   boneless, skinless chicken breast halves
½   cup green onions, thinly sliced
¼   pound mushrooms, thinly sliced
1   tablespoon butter or margarine
3   tablespoons flour
¼   teaspoon thyme leaves
½   cup chicken broth
½   cup milk
½   cup dry white wine
     salt and pepper to taste
¾   cup crab meat or 6½-ounces canned crab meat
⅓   cup finely chopped parsley
⅓   cup dry bread crumbs
1   cup shredded Swiss cheese

- Pound chicken breasts until ¼-inch thick.
- Sauté onions and mushrooms in butter or margarine until juices evaporate. Stir in flour and thyme. Blend in broth, milk and wine. Cook, stirring, until sauce thickens. Season to taste with salt and pepper.
- Stir together ¼ cup sauce, crab, parsley and crumbs. Spoon crab filling on each chicken breast and wrap chicken around filling.
- Spray a baking pan well with non-stick cooking spray. Place chicken , seam side down in the pan. Pour remaining sauce over chicken. Top with cheese. Cover and bake at 350 degrees for 30 to 40 minutes.

GINGER CHICKEN

3   *whole chicken breasts split in half, or 1 frying chicken, cut-up*

2   *tablespoons peeled and finely diced ginger root*

1   *tablespoon oil*

1½ *tablespoons lemon juice*

1   *small onion, chopped*

1   *tablespoon honey*

1   *clove garlic, minced*

½   *teaspoon ground coriander*

¼   *teaspoon ground cumin*

½   *teaspoon salt or to taste*

1   *lemon*
    parsley or cilantro

- Remove skin and fat from chicken.
- Put remaining ingredients, except lemon and parsley or cilantro, in a blender and whirl a few seconds. Pour over the chicken. Cover and refrigerate overnight. Turn occasionally.
- Place in a single layer in a shallow baking dish and bake at 350 degrees for 20 minutes.
- Place under the broiler for 3 minutes or until the chicken is browned. Garnish with lemon slices and chopped parsley or cilantro.

Stir-fry Chinese vegetables or a vegetable curry go well with this low-fat dish.

ORANGE CHICKEN WITH ONION MARMALADE

Serves 2

2 boneless, skinless chicken breast halves
3 tablespoons orange juice
1 teaspoon lemon juice
2 teaspoons grated fresh ginger root
1 small garlic clove, peeled and minced
1 teaspoon olive oil
   salt and freshly ground pepper to taste

Onion Marmalade

1 tablespoon golden raisins
1 tablespoon lemon juice
1 tablespoon orange juice
2 teaspoons olive oil
1 medium yellow onion, peeled and thinly sliced
1 tablespoon grated fresh ginger
¼ teaspoon salt or to taste
   pinch of paprika
   pinch of cayenne pepper
2 teaspoons honey

- Combine the chicken with orange and lemon juices, ginger and garlic in a non-metallic pan; refrigerate at least 1 hour.
- Combine the raisins and lemon and orange juices. Set aside about 10 minutes.
- Heat the oil in a large skillet over medium-low heat. Add onion and sauté until very soft and light golden in color, about 20 minutes. Add the raisin mixture, ginger, salt, paprika and cayenne. Cook about 2 minutes more or until liquid has thickened and is coating the onions. Remove from heat and stir in honey.
- Heat 1 teaspoon olive oil in a large non-stick skillet over medium-high heat. Scrape garlic and ginger from chicken and discard; cook the breasts about 4 to 5 minutes on each side or until juices run clear and pieces are nicely browned. Reduce heat, if needed, to prevent burning. Add salt and pepper.
- Serve chicken with the warm marmalade on top.

BASIL AND LEMON CHICKEN

Serves 4

1   *3½ pound chicken, quartered*

Marinade

½   *cup fresh lemon juice*
½   *cup light clover honey*
¼   *cup olive oil*
2   *cloves garlic, chopped*
½   *cup finely chopped fresh basil*
½   *teaspoon coarse black pepper*

Fresh Basil Salsa

2   *cups peeled, seeded and diced cucumber*
1½   *cups coarsely chopped fresh basil*
     finely grated rind of 1 lemon
     freshly ground black pepper to taste
2   *tablespoons fresh lemon juice*

~ Clean chicken well. Remove backbone, then flatten breastbone. Place chicken quarters in a non-metallic dish.

~ Combine lemon juice, honey, oil and garlic in a blender. Process about 30 seconds. Remove to a bowl, stir in basil and pepper, and pour over chicken. Cover and refrigerate at least 6 hours or overnight; turn a few times to coat.

~ Remove chicken from marinade. Place leg and thigh pieces 3 to 4 inches from hot coals and grill for 10 minutes, turning once. Add breast to grill and cook 30 minutes more, turning and basting the chicken every 10 minutes.

~ Salsa: Mix cucumber, basil, lemon rind and pepper. Fifteen minutes before serving, toss with lemon juice and mix well. Serve salsa over the grilled chicken.

Remember, any recipe that calls for a grill can also work well with a broiler! This salsa is good with grilled fish, also.

ALMOND CRUSTED CHICKEN

Serves 4

½ *cup ground almonds, lightly toasted*
1 *cup fine, white bread crumbs*
   salt to taste
   pepper or lemon pepper
4 *boned chicken pieces (breasts or thighs)*
2 *egg whites, lightly whipped*

- Blend almonds, bread crumbs, salt and pepper together.
- Pound each chicken piece to uniform thickness, about ¼-inch. Dip in egg whites and roll in crumb mixture. Press crumbs into the meat lightly to help them adhere. Refrigerate 1 to 2 hours to firm the crust.
- Spray a shallow pan with non-stick spray. Arrange chicken pieces in the pan. Bake, uncovered, at 350 degrees for 15 to 20 minutes or until done. Do not turn the chicken during baking.

Also good cold on a Kaiser roll.

ROAST CHICKEN IN PORT

Serves 4

1   *tablespoon butter or margarine*

3   *tablespoons vegetable oil*

1   *clove garlic, crushed*

1   *4 to 5 pound roasting chicken*
    salt and pepper

4   *tablespoons cognac, divided*

⅓   *cup port*

½   *cup chicken broth*

½   *teaspoon dried basil*

½   *teaspoon dried thyme*

≈ Heat the butter or margarine and oil in a medium-sized roasting pan or casserole on top of the stove. Add garlic. Brown chicken over medium heat for about 10 minutes. Remove chicken and most of the oil from the pan. Place chicken on a rack and return to the roasting pan. Salt and pepper to taste.

≈ Mix together 3 tablespoons cognac, port, broth, basil and thyme in a small saucepan. Heat to simmer and pour over the chicken. Roast uncovered at 350 degrees for 20 minutes per pound, basting often.

≈ Place chicken on a serving platter and keep warm. Strain as much of the grease from the roasting pan as possible. Add the remaining 1 tablespoon of the cognac to the pan and boil the sauce until it is reduced to about ½ cup and is slightly thickened.

≈ Cut the chicken into serving-size pieces. Pour the port sauce over the chicken and serve.

Today's roasting chicken is not yesterday's old fat hen!

CHICKEN FAJITAS

Serves 4 to 6

3   tablespoons fresh lime juice
2   teaspoons vegetable oil
1   large clove garlic, minced
    salt to taste
½   teaspoon freshly ground black pepper
1   tablespoon minced fresh cilantro
1½ pounds boneless, skinless chicken, cut in thin strips
1   medium red bell pepper, cut in thin strips
1 to 2 jalapeno peppers, seeded and cut in thin strips
3   green onions, sliced
1   package flour tortillas
½   head romaine lettuce, coarsely shredded
2   large tomatoes, cut into wedges
½   lime, cut into wedges
    shredded Cheddar cheese for topping
    avocado slices
½   cup prepared salsa

- Stir together lime juice, 1 teaspoon oil, garlic, salt, pepper and cilantro. Put chicken in a glass bowl. Add lime juice mixture and marinate, covered, in the refrigerator for at least 2 hours.

- In a large skillet, heat the remaining teaspoon of oil over medium-high heat. Add the peppers and green onions. Stir fry for 2 minutes. Remove from pan.

- Place pan back over medium-high to high heat. Add drained chicken and stir fry for 3 minutes. Chicken should be seared on the outside. If chicken steams instead of browning, cook in 3 small batches instead. Return vegetables to the pan and cook 1 minute more to blend flavors and heat completely.

- Heat tortillas by slitting the package and heating it on high for 1 minute in the microwave or individual tortillas can be heated, wrapped in a paper towel, for 6 to 7 seconds each.

- Place shredded lettuce on a large serving platter and top with the hot chicken mixture. Surround with tomato and lime wedges. Serve with tortillas, shredded cheese, sliced avocado and salsa.

CHICKEN TAMALE PIE

Serves 6

4   cups chopped fresh ripe tomatoes, or 1 28-ounce
     can Italian-style plum tomatoes with juice
1   16-ounce can cream-style corn
1   teaspoon salt or to taste
1   medium onion, chopped
½   cup olive oil
1½ tablespoon chili powder, or to taste
¼   cup chopped celery
¼   cup chopped green pepper
¼   cup sliced fresh mushrooms
1   garlic clove, minced
1   cup low-fat milk
½   cup yellow cornmeal
3   eggs, lightly beaten
1   cup pitted ripe olives
2   cups coarsely chopped cooked chicken
1   cup shredded Monterey Jack cheese, mixed with
1   cup shredded sharp Cheddar cheese
     olive oil for drizzling
     Pineapple Salsa (see Salsas, Chutneys and
     Preserves)

❧ Combine tomatoes, corn, salt, onion, olive oil, chili powder, celery, green pepper, mushrooms and garlic in a large saucepan and cook over medium heat for 15 minutes.

❧ Stir together milk, cornmeal and eggs. Add to tomato mixture and cook, stirring constantly to prevent scorching, until thick, about 15 minutes. Remove from heat and stir in olives and chicken.

❧ Pour mixture into a lightly greased shallow baking dish. Sprinkle with cheeses, drizzle with oil and bake at 350 degrees until pie is firm and the cheese is crusty, about 35 to 40 minutes. Serve piping hot with Pineapple Salsa on the side.

This recipe has been a big hit at potluck dinners.

TURKEY SLICES À LA MARSALA

Serves 6

2 turkey breasts, thinly sliced
   salt and pepper to taste
2 tablespoons olive oil (more if needed)
1 tablespoon butter
1 medium onion, chopped
3 tablespoons chopped fresh parsley
   juice of 1 lemon
1 cup Marsala wine

- Tenderize the turkey slices slightly with a wooden mallet. Salt and pepper the slices and brown on both sides in olive oil and butter. Remove turkey from pan.

- Sauté the onion and parsley in the same pan for about a minute; add lemon juice and wine and stir well. Return turkey to the pan; cover and simmer until turkey is tender, about 20 minutes.

RASPBERRY-GLAZED TURKEY TENDERLOINS

Serves 6 to 8

½ cup seedless raspberry jam
6 tablespoons raspberry vinegar
¼ cup Dijon mustard
1 teaspoon grated orange peel
½ teaspoon dried thyme leaves
4 turkey breast tenderloins (about 2¼ pounds total)

- Stir together jam, vinegar, mustard, orange peel and thyme in a 1 to 2 quart pan. Bring to a boil over high heat and cook, stirring, until reduced by about a fourth (2 to 3 minutes). Reserve about ½ cup of the glaze; brush turkey with some of the remaining glaze.

- Place turkey on a rack in a broiler pan. Broil about 4 inches below heat, turning and brushing once with remaining glaze, until meat in center is no longer pink, about 8 to 10 minutes.

- Slice crosswise. Serve with reserved glaze.

TURKEY SAUSAGE AND PEPPERS

Serves 2

½ *pound (4 links) Italian-style turkey sausage*
½ *cup water, or more if necessary*
½ *cup thinly sliced yellow onion*
½ *cup thinly sliced fennel bulb*
½ *cup thinly sliced red bell pepper*
½ *cup thinly sliced yellow bell pepper*
2 *green onions, minced*

🍂 Cook the sausage in ½ cup of the water in a covered skillet over moderate heat for 20 minutes.

🍂 Add onion, fennel, and peppers. Increase heat to moderately high and sauté, stirring frequently, for 20 minutes or until vegetables are tender. Add more water if necessary to keep the mixture from sticking.

🍂 Sprinkle with green onions and serve.

TURKEY LOAF

Serves 8

1½ *pounds ground turkey*
½ *cup diced green bell pepper*
½ *cup diced yellow onion*
½ *cup seasoned bread crumbs*
¼ *cup thinly sliced green onions*
2 *teaspoons minced garlic*
2 *eggs*
¼ *cup chili sauce*
¼ *cup skim milk*
½ *teaspoon ground cumin*
¼ *teaspoon ground nutmeg*
¼ *teaspoon freshly ground black pepper*
⅛ *teaspoon cayenne pepper*

🍂 Combine turkey, green pepper, onion, bread crumbs, green onions and garlic.

🍂 In another bowl, combine egg, chili sauce, milk, cumin, nutmeg, black pepper and cayenne pepper. Add to turkey mixture and combine thoroughly.

🍂 Form a round loaf 7 inches across. Bake at 375 degrees for 50 minutes.

🍂 While loaf bakes, mix salsa ingredients. Set aside.

🍂 Let cooked loaf stand for 10 minutes before slicing. Serve topped with tomato salsa.

Tomato Salsa

2 *cups chopped plum tomatoes*
1 *cup coarsely sliced green onions*
¼ *cup chopped fresh cilantro*
1 *tablespoon olive oil*

ROCK CORNISH GAME HEN WITH WILD RICE

Serves 6

6 Cornish game hens
 salt and pepper to taste
3 garlic cloves, cut in halves
½ cup melted butter or margarine
¾ cup red currant jelly
3 tablespoons port wine

Wild Rice

6 oz. wild rice
2 tablespoons oil or butter
½ pound mushrooms
½ cup minced onion
¼ cup chopped celery
½ teaspoon dried thyme
½ teaspoon powdered sage
2 tablespoons chopped parsley

- Sprinkle the cavity of each game hen with salt and pepper. Put ½ clove of garlic in each. Place in a shallow roasting pan. Sprinkle with salt and pepper. Drizzle with melted butter or margarine. Roast uncovered at 400 degrees for 1 hour, basting often with pan drippings.
- Heat currant jelly with the port wine on low heat.
- Drain the pan juices from the roaster. Pour jelly and port glaze over game hens and continue roasting for 15 minutes longer, brushing often with the glaze.
- Arrange on a bed of wild rice and serve.

Wild Rice

- Cook rice according to package directions.
- Slice mushrooms if large and sauté with onions, celery, thyme, sage and parsley. Cook until softened. Add to the cooked, warm wild rice.

This recipe may be reduced easily by ⅓ for 2 servings. Also, long grain rice may be substituted for the wild rice, allowing ⅓ cup cooked per person.

BRAISED DUCK IN SOY SAUCE

Serves 6

1   *4-pound duck*

1   *tablespoon vegetable oil*

2½   *cups cold water*

½   *cup reduced sodium soy sauce*

4   *green onions with tops cut in half*

3   *slices ginger root, ½-inch thick*

3   *tablespoons dry sherry*

2   *whole star anise*

½   *stick cinnamon*

1   *tablespoon granulated sugar*

1   *teaspoon to 1 tablespoon sesame oil, as taste
    indicates
    lettuce leaves and tomato wedges*

ꙮ Rinse duck and pat dry with paper towels.

ꙮ Heat oil in a large, heavy saucepan or Dutch oven
over medium-high heat. Brown duck on both sides
in hot oil. Drain off as much oil as possible before
proceeding.

ꙮ Slowly add water, soy sauce, onions, ginger, sherry,
anise and cinnamon. Bring to a boil; lower heat and
simmer, covered, 2½ hours. Turn duck twice during
cooking period.

ꙮ Remove duck and keep warm.

ꙮ Skim all excess fat from the liquid. Over medium-
high heat reduce to 1¼ cups. Stir in sugar and
sesame oil to taste.

ꙮ Place duck on lettuce-lined platter. Pour sauce over
the duck and garnish with tomato wedges and serve.

*Plain steamed rice is a good
accompaniment for this special
entrée.*

*Mix equal parts of regular soy
sauce and water for a measure of
soy sauce. The flavor will be better
and sodium will be less than so-
called "light soy." Better yet, mix
soy and sherry, half and half!*

FIN FISH

❧

SHELL FISH

SOUSED HALIBUT

Serves 4 to 5

2   pounds halibut fillets
2   tablespoons butter, margarine or oil
⅓   cup olive or salad oil
1½ tablespoons vinegar
¼   cup orange juice
2   teaspoons salt
¼   teaspoon cayenne
2   tablespoons slivered orange zest
2   tablespoons slivered green or red pepper
2   tablespoons minced green onion
    thickly cut chilled unpeeled orange slices

- Sauté fillets in butter, margarine or oil until just lightly brown but not cooked through, and arrange carefully in a flat dish, keeping them whole. Marinade will complete the cooking process.
- Marinade: Make a sauce with oil, vinegar, orange juice, orange zest, green or red pepper and green onion. Pour over fish and let stand in the refrigerator for 6 to 8 hours, or longer, basting the fish with the sauce once or twice.
- Serve cold with orange slices.

Wonderful on a warm summer evening.

HALIBUT IN FRESH TOMATO CURRY

Serves 3 to 4

1 to 2 tablespoons butter or vegetable oil
2   cloves garlic, crushed
1   medium onion, sliced into thin wedges
1   bay leaf
4   tomatoes, sliced into wedges or 1 15-ounce can chopped tomatoes in sauce
¼   cup raisins
1 to 2 teaspoons curry powder or to taste
1½ pounds halibut steaks

- In a heavy skillet, heat 1 tablespoon butter or oil over medium heat until foamy. Add garlic and brown on all sides; reduce heat and add onions and bay leaf. Cook, stirring several times, until onions are soft.
- Add tomatoes, cook for 3 minutes; add raisins and curry powder.
- Slide halibut into bubbling sauce, partially cover pan, and poach until opaque and firm (This may take from 12 to 20 minutes, depending on thickness of steak.)
- Remove and discard bay leaf and garlic. Serve halibut with sauce surrounding it.

HALIBUT CHEEKS

Serves 4

1½   pounds fresh halibut cheeks
3 to 4   green onions, chopped
½   teaspoon grated fresh ginger
1   tablespoon vegetable oil
8 to 12   drops sesame oil

- Make 4 individual parchment or foil squares and divide halibut among them. Mix together green onions, ginger, vegetable oil and sesame oil. Divide evenly among halibut packages. Fold each bundle to seal.
- Bake at 375 degrees for 15 to 18 minutes.

Optional additions might be pea pods, mushrooms, thinly sliced carrots or slim stalks of asparagus.

SWORDFISH WITH MUSHROOM AND TOMATO SAUCE *Serves 4*

   butter-flavored vegetable cooking spray
2   teaspoons margarine
4   4-ounce swordfish steaks (¾-inch thick)
2   cups coarsely chopped fresh shiitake mushrooms
½   cup seeded, chopped tomato
¼   cup chopped green onions
¼   cup dry white wine
¼   cup clam juice or an additional ¼ cup wine
2   tablespoons tomato paste
2   teaspoons minced garlic
1   teaspoon minced fresh thyme
¼   teaspoon ground cumin
1   tablespoon lemon juice

- Coat a large non-stick skillet with cooking spray; add margarine. Place over medium heat until hot. Add swordfish and cook 3 minutes on each side; set aside and keep warm. Wipe skillet dry with a paper towel.
- Coat skillet with cooking spray. Add mushrooms and sauté 1 minute. Add tomato and next 7 ingredients, stirring well. Top with fish; cover and cook over medium heat 5 minutes or until fish flakes easily when tested with a fork.
- Transfer fish to a serving platter. Stir lemon juice into tomato mixture and spoon over fish. Serve immediately.

Great with halibut!

SOUFFLÉD SALMON STEAKS

Serves 6

¼ cup margarine, melted
2 tablespoons dry white wine
6 salmon steaks, 1-inch thick or 6 salmon fillets
3 egg whites at room temperature
½ cup mayonnaise
2 tablespoons green onion slices
½ teaspoon dry mustard

- Combine margarine and wine.
- Place fish on greased rack of broiler pan. Broil 6 to 8 minutes on each side until fish flakes easily with fork, brushing frequently with margarine mixture.
- Beat egg whites until stiff peaks form; fold in mayonnaise, onion and mustard. Spoon onto fish; broil until lightly browned.

A dramatic way to serve salmon! Also works well with halibut steaks, but the color contrast is best with salmon.

GRILLED SALMON WITH SAGE

Serves 4 to 6

1 salmon fillet, 2 to 3 pounds
2 tablespoons fresh lime juice
1½ teaspoons ground sage
1 tablespoon butter, margarine or canola oil

- Place fish on foil, sprinkle with lemon, sage and butter.
- Bake in 350 degree oven 15 minutes or until salmon just flakes.

Barbeque, broil or bake salmon fillet to perfection. Nothing could be simpler. In late summer serve with corn on the cob and baked Walla Walla onions.

SALMON TART

Serves 6

Parmesan Crust

- 1½   cups unbleached flour
- 2   ounces grated Asiago, Romano or Parmesan cheese (½ cup)
- ⅓   cup canola oil
- ¼   cup non-fat milk

Filling

- 1   large onion, diced
- 1   tablespoon margarine
- 1   pound salmon, cooked, deboned and flaked
- 2-3   garlic cloves, minced
- 1   16-ounce carton plain non-fat yogurt
- 1   egg plus 4 egg whites slightly beaten, or 5 - 6 egg whites only
- 4   ounces (1 cup) shredded reduced-fat Swiss cheese
- 1   teaspoon dill weed, crumbled
  salt to taste

Crust

- ✎ Combine the flour and cheese.
- ✎ In a separate bowl mix oil and milk until creamy.
- ✎ Pour liquid mixture into the flour mixture and blend with a fork.
- ✎ Pat the dough with your fingers into a 9-inch deep-dish pie or quiche pan, pressing into the bottom and up the sides.
- ✎ Bake at 375 degrees for 10 minutes.

Filling

- ✎ Cook the onion in the margarine until softened.
- ✎ Combine all ingredients and pour into baked crust.
- ✎ Bake at 375 degrees for 45-50 minutes.
- ✎ Cool in pan for 15 minutes before serving.

In Puget Sound country we have fresh salmon available year round. Poach fresh salmon or plan to have some left over in the freezer. Canned salmon may be used, and the results will be almost as good. This is also excellent served cold.

GRILLED FISH WITH HERBS

Serves 4

   1   tablespoon olive oil
   2   tablespoons lime or lemon juice
  ½   cup dry white wine
  ½   teaspoon dry mustard
   1   teaspoon chili powder
   1   teaspoon pepper
   4   tablespoons fresh cilantro, finely chopped
 1½   pound firm white fish steaks, such as halibut,
       lingcod, swordfish, or salmon

- Combine olive oil, lime juice and wine in bowl. Add spices.
- Pour marinade over fish steaks and marinate 15-20 minutes.
- Grill fish over hot coals, about 5 minutes per side, or until fish turns opaque. Baste with marinade while cooking.

Can also be baked in a 350 degree oven for 15 to 20 minutes.

BLACK COD IN AVOCADO SAUCE

   1   avocado, peeled and cut into slices
   2   tablespoons juice
   1   teaspoon grated lemon peel
  ½   cup fresh cilantro (or 2 teaspoons dried)
 2-3   cloves garlic, minced
       olive oil
  ¼   cup pine nuts
  ⅓   teaspoon freshly grated nutmeg
 8-12 ounces black cod fillets or 2 cod steaks

- Put avocado, lemon juice, rind and garlic in food processor and blend for 1 minute.
- Add 1 tablespoon of olive oil if necessary. Stir in pine nuts and nutmeg.
- Place fish in baking dish and cover with sauce.
- Bake at 350 degrees for 20 minutes.

TUNA STEAKS SICILIAN

Serves 6

olive oil-flavored vegetable cooking spray
3 garlic cloves, minced
1 8-ounce can tomato sauce
2 cups chopped plum tomatoes (about 4 medium)
¼ cup chopped fresh parsley
½ teaspoon dried whole oregano
¼ teaspoon crushed red pepper flakes
2 12-ounce tuna steaks 1-inch thick
¼ cup sliced pimiento-stuffed olives
2 tablespoons capers
   fresh parsley sprigs (optional)

- Coat a large non-stick skillet with cooking spray; place over medium-high heat until hot. Add garlic and sauté until lightly browned. Add tomato sauce and next 4 ingredients; stir well. Reduce heat and simmer, uncovered, 5 minutes.

- Spoon half of tomato mixture into an 11x7x2-inch baking dish; place tuna steaks on tomato mixture. Spoon remaining tomato mixture evenly over steaks. Sprinkle evenly with olives and capers. Cover and bake at 350 degrees for 40 minutes or until fish flakes easily when tested with a fork.

- Transfer to a serving platter. Garnish with fresh parsley sprigs, if desired.

RED SNAPPER IN WINE SAUCE

Serves 3 to 4

1 green onion, chopped
¼ cup chopped red bell pepper
1 garlic clove, minced
2 tablespoons raisins
¼ teaspoon ground cinnamon
¾ cup white wine or chicken broth
½ cup frozen petite peas
1 pound red snapper fillets

- Combine all ingredients except fish and mix well. Pour over fish in baking pan, cover and bake five minutes at 450 degrees.

- Remove cover and spoon sauce over fish. Bake five minutes longer.

Good served with rice or orzo.

Baked Fish Greek Style

Serves 4 to 6

2½ pounds salmon or halibut
    salt and pepper to taste
  1 can (8 ounces) tomato sauce
 ½ cup dry white wine
  3 tablespoons fresh lemon juice
3 or 4 cloves garlic, minced
 ½ cup chopped parsley
  1 pound (3 or 4) fresh tomatoes
 ½ cup bread crumbs
 ⅓ cup olive oil

- Place fish in a 10x8-inch baking dish. Sprinkle with salt and pepper.
- Combine tomato sauce, wine and lemon juice; pour over fish. Sprinkle with garlic and parsley.
- Cut tomatoes in thin slices; arrange over fish. Sprinkle with bread crumbs; drizzle with olive oil. Bake at 350 degrees for 25 minutes. Baste often during last half of cooking time to form a nice golden crust.

Serve with crusty sourdough bread.

Monkfish with Mustard Sauce

Serves 6

  3 tablespoons olive oil
2¼ pounds monkfish
  3 tablespoons Dijon mustard
 ⅓ cup chopped shallots
½ to 1 tablespoon minced garlic
 ¼ pound small mushrooms; large ones should be sliced if used
  2 tablespoons dry white wine or chicken broth
    fresh parsley or other fresh herb for garnish

- Pour olive oil into baking dish. Turn fillets over in oil to coat. Brush with mustard and sprinkle with shallots, garlic and mushrooms.
- Bake for 15 minutes in a 375 degree oven. Add wine and bake another 5 to 8 minutes. Serve with the sauce from the pan.

Good with rice and black beans or couscous.

FILLET OF SOLE WITH ROSEMARY AND BASIL

Serves 4

3 shallots, chopped

1½ pounds thin sole or flounder fillets

3 tablespoons chopped fresh basil

1 tablespoon chopped fresh rosemary, or ½ teaspoon
   dried rosemary
   freshly ground black pepper to taste

4 tablespoons white wine

3 tablespoons lemon juice

2 tablespoons chopped fresh sorrel or parsley for
   garnish

- Spray a 9x12-inch baking dish with non-stick cooking spray. Sprinkle shallots over the bottom.

- Season fish with herbs and pepper. Starting with the short end, loosely roll each fillet into a cylinder and place the rolls, seam side down, in the baking dish. Pour wine and lemon juice over the fish and bake in a 350 degree oven for about 20 minutes, basting occasionally with the liquid. Remove from the oven and sprinkle with the chopped sorrel or parsley before serving.

Great way to use the skinny fillets of Dover sole! Serve with rice.

Halibut, lingcod, orange roughy, salmon, snapper and swordfish as well as many other fish are interchangeable in most recipes. Keep in mind that snapper is the least firm.

SOLE FILLET FILO PACKETS

Serves 4

½ *8-ounce package Neufchatel cheese, softened*
2 *ounces goat cheese, softened*
1 *tablespoon chopped fresh chives*
2 *teaspoons fresh lemon juice*
4 *sheets filo pastry*
   butter-flavored vegetable cooking spray
4 *3-ounce sole fillets*
   fresh chives (optional)
   lemon slices (optional)

- Combine first four ingredients in a small bowl. Stir well and set aside.
- Place 1 sheet of filo on a damp towel (keep remaining filo covered). Lightly coat filo with cooking spray; fold in half crosswise. Spread ¼ of cheese mixture across bottom 2 inches of filo and place 1 fillet on filo above cheese mixture. Fold cheese-covered filo over fish; fold lengthwise edges in about 1 inch and roll up, jelly roll fashion.
- Lightly coat filo packet with cooking spray and place on a baking sheet coated with cooking spray. Repeat procedure with remaining filo, cheese mixture, and fillets.
- Bake at 375 degrees for 20 minutes. Transfer to a serving platter. If desired, garnish with fresh chives and lemon slices. Serve immediately.

An easy and elegant company dish. May be prepared ahead and refrigerated 2 to 3 hours. Bake an additional 5 minutes if chilled.

All but the very thin fish fillets may be baked, broiled, pan fried, or barbecued regardless of the method suggested in the recipe. Microwaving is the fastest but ovens vary so much that it is difficult to spell out exact cooking times.

FISH DU JOUR

Serves 3 to 4

1½   *pounds fish fillets or steaks about 1-inch thick,*
      such as cod, halibut, lingcod, snapper or
      swordfish.
½ *to* ¾ *cup yogurt and seasonings of choice from one of*
      the groups below
fresh bread crumbs

- Bake fish for 10 minutes in a 350 degree oven.
- Mix yogurt and seasonings. Cover fish with seasoned yogurt and bread crumbs and bake 8 to 10 minutes longer.

Seasoning Suggestions

- Curry powder, garlic and cumin.
- Sesame seed, soy sauce, ginger and green onion.
- Tarragon, parsley, white Worcestershire sauce, and black pepper
- Chili powder or cumin and salsa
- Garlic, oregano and black pepper
- Green onion, sliced mushrooms and celery seed
- Chopped tomato, green onion and feta or gorgonzola cheese
- Chopped tomato, green onion, paprika, cilantro, and orange juice
- Chopped red pepper, garlic, dry mustard, hot pepper seasoning and red wine vinegar
- Honey, mustard, green taco seasoning

This is simply a basic recipe to bake fish, using a yogurt sauce, with whatever seasonings appeal to you. Suggestions for the seasonings are given without quantities so that you can please your own palate.

SEAFOOD LASAGNA

Serves 10 to 12

2   tablespoons butter or margarine

¾   cup finely chopped onion

3   garlic cloves, minced

1   pound raw shrimp, peeled and cut into small
     pieces

1   pound scallops, cut into small pieces if large

½   cup dry white wine, vermouth or chicken broth

2   cups thinly sliced mushrooms

1   cup crushed canned tomatoes

¼   teaspoon crushed hot red pepper flakes

3   tablespoons finely chopped fresh parsley

½   teaspoon dried oregano

½   teaspoon dried basil
     salt and pepper to taste

2½ cups evaporated skim milk or light cream

3   tablespoons flour

9   lasagna noodles

1½ pounds thin sole fillets

1½ cups grated Swiss cheese

½   cup grated Asiago or Romano cheese

*Wonderful during the holidays
with a green salad and a mince
pie. May be assembled and cooked
later. Also, layering in the exact
order is not necessary, just be sure
to end with sauce and cheese on
top. Dividing the recipe in half
works well, too!*

- Heat butter in large skillet. Add onions and garlic and cook 2 to 3 minutes. Add shrimp and scallops and cook until shrimp begin to turn pink. Using a slotted spoon, transfer the seafood to a bowl.
- Add wine to the liquid in the pan and bring to a boil; add mushrooms and cook 5 minutes. Add tomatoes and cook an additional 5 minutes. Add pepper flakes, parsley, oregano, basil and salt and pepper.
- Blend evaporated milk with the flour. Slowly add to the sauce. Add any liquid that has accumulated in the bowl of seafood to the sauce and cook until thickened.
- Cook noodles according to package directions and drain well.
- Spray a 9x13-inch baking dish with a cooking spray. Spoon a layer of sauce over the bottom of the pan. Add half of the seafood, cover with more of the sauce and lay three of the lasagna noodles over the sauce. Place the sole fillets on top and cover with a light layer of sauce and top with three more strips of lasagna noodles. Scatter remaining seafood, spoon a light layer of sauce next and place the final three lasagna noodles on top. Spoon the remaining sauce over the top and sprinkle the cheese over all.
- Bake at 375 degrees for 30 to 45 minutes or until hot and bubbly.

SEAFOOD WITH PUFF PASTRY CRUST

Serves 6 to 8

1 medium onion, chopped

1 rib of celery, thinly sliced

2 to 3 garlic cloves, minced

2 tablespoons olive oil

½ teaspoon fennel seeds

1 cup wine or chicken broth

1 14-ounce can diced tomatoes, including the juice
red pepper sauce to taste

⅓ pound mushrooms, quartered

1 pound red potatoes, peeled and cut into small cubes

½ teaspoon dried thyme

½ teaspoon dried basil

½ cup evaporated skim milk or cream

3 tablespoons cornstarch

1½ pounds firm-textured fish such as monkfish, halibut, swordfish or lingcod, cut into 1-inch pieces

½ pound fresh scallops, cut into small pieces if large

1 pound fresh shrimp, shelled and cut in half

2 tablespoons chopped fresh parsley

1 sheet of frozen puff pastry, thawed

🍂 Cook onion, celery and garlic in oil over moderately low heat until onion is soft but not brown. Add fennel seeds, broth, tomatoes, red pepper sauce, mushrooms, potatoes, thyme and basil; simmer covered until potatoes are barely done.

🍂 Combine milk and cornstarch and stir into potato mixture. Bring to a boil, stirring constantly. Stir in the fish, seafood and parsley and transfer to a three quart baking dish.

🍂 Roll out pastry to fit the baking dish and place over the casserole. Bake at 425 degrees for 17 to 20 minutes.

🍂 To serve, cut the crust into 6 to 8 pieces and place on plates. Spoon fish and sauce over the pastry.

May be assembled and baked later.

SEAFOOD IN FILO PASTRY

Serves 6 to 8

   2   tablespoons butter
   ½   cup thinly sliced celery
   ½   cup chopped onion
   1   cup sliced mushrooms
   4   tablespoons flour
   1   teaspoon salt
 1½   cups milk
   ½   cup vermouth or white wine
   2   tablespoons lemon juice
   ⅓   cup grated Asiago or Parmesan cheese
   ½   pound cooked shrimp
   ½   pound cooked sole, flaked
   1   pound cooked fresh salmon, flaked
   8   sheets filo pastry
   ¾   cup melted butter or use non-stick cooking spray
        and 2 tablespoons melted butter

- Heat butter and cook celery and onion until tender. Add mushrooms and cook five minutes.
- Sift in flour along with salt, if desired. Add milk slowly and cook until slightly thickened. Stir in wine, lemon juice and cheese. Cook and stir constantly until thick. Remove from heat and stir in shrimp, sole and salmon.
- Brush each sheet of pastry with melted butter or spray with cooking spray and lay one on top of another in a greased 9x13-inch baking dish. Spoon seafood mixture down the middle of the pastry. Fold both sides in so they overlap. Flip gently so seam is facing down. Tuck ends under and brush with remaining butter.
- Bake at 375 degrees 35 to 40 minutes or until crisp and golden brown.

Makes an elegant first course or luncheon dish as well as a dinner entree.

SQUID MARINARA WITH LINGUINE

Serves 6 to 8

2 tablespoons olive oil

1 medium onion, coarsely chopped

2 to 4 garlic cloves, minced

2 pounds plum tomatoes, pureed in blender or food processor or 1 1-pound 12-ounce can diced tomatoes in sauce

2 tablespoons sun-dried tomato paste

6 fresh basil leaves, chopped, or ½ teaspoon dried

2 teaspoons fresh oregano, chopped or 1 teaspoon dried

⅛ teaspoon cayenne

½ bay leaf

½ teaspoon black pepper

½ cup water

2 pounds squid, cleaned and sliced into rings

1 pound linguine or thin spaghetti
   grated Parmesan or Romano

🍃 Heat oil over medium heat and cook onion and garlic until soft, about 2 minutes. Add tomatoes, tomato paste, herbs and peppers. Simmer 15 minutes, stirring occasionally. Add water and simmer a few minutes longer.

🍃 Add squid to sauce and simmer 8 to 10 minutes more.

🍃 Cook linguine according to package directions and drain.

🍃 Serve linguine with sauce spooned over it. Sprinkle cheese over the top.

Good served with either garlic bread or thick slices of Italian bread brushed with olive oil.

SCALLOPS WITH CURRY

Serves 2

¾ pound scallops

1 tablespoon fresh lemon juice

2 tablespoons honey

1 to 2 teaspoons curry powder or to taste

🍃 Place scallops in individual ramekins or oven proof casserole.

🍃 Mix lemon juice, honey and curry and pour over scallops. Bake at 400 degrees for 10 minutes.

Try this recipe with Arboretum Honey from our gift shop!

TROPICAL BARBECUED SHRIMP

Serves 4 to 6

2 pounds fresh shrimp
¾ cup frozen orange juice concentrate, thawed
2 tablespoons vinegar, preferably fruit vinegar
1½ teaspoons minced fresh ginger
2 tablespoons brown sugar or molasses
2 tablespoons minced fresh basil or 2 teaspoons dried

◆ Peel shrimp, leaving tail on, and devein.

◆ Combine orange juice, vinegar, ginger, sugar or molasses and basil. Blend well. Add shrimp and marinate for 1 hour in refrigerator.

◆ Place on 4 to 6 skewers and barbecue or broil for 7 to 8 minutes, turning once, until shrimp are cooked. Baste occasionally with marinade. Serve with rice and a green vegetable.

Shrimp may be baked in the sauce for 10 minutes at 400 degrees.

BAKED SHRIMP

Serves 4 to 5

1½ pounds fresh shrimp
3 tablespoons olive oil
1½ tablespoons minced shallots or green onion
2 garlic cloves, minced
2 teaspoons fresh herbs, such as basil, tarragon or rosemary
½ cup fresh bread crumbs
3 tablespoons grated Parmesan or Asiago cheese

◆ Peel and devein shrimp, leaving tails on. Butterfly by slicing underside not quite all the way through and flatten.

◆ Blend olive oil, shallots, garlic, fresh herbs, bread crumbs and cheese and press filling into each shrimp.

◆ Place on a lightly greased baking sheet and bake at 425 degrees for 8 to 10 minutes, or until shrimp are pink and stuffing is lightly browned.

MUSSELS AND PASTA IN PESTO SAUCE

Serves 4 to 5

1½ pound mussels
1 tablespoon plus 1 teaspoon olive oil
2 garlic cloves, minced
1 bunch fresh basil, chopped
2 tablespoons grated Parmesan cheese, divided
2 tablespoons pine nuts, toasted and divided
½ cup dry white wine
8 ounces fresh shell pasta or 4 ounces dry

- Scrub mussels and debeard them.
- Steam mussels for 6 to 8 minutes, discarding any that fail to open.
- In blender or food processor, combine 1 tablespoon olive oil, garlic, basil, 1 tablespoon cheese, 1 tablespoon pine nuts and wine. Blend to a smooth, thin paste, adding up to ¼ cup water if needed.
- Cook pasta in boiling water according to package directions.
- While pasta is cooking, heat shelled mussels in remaining oil for 3 to 4 minutes; add pesto sauce and simmer mussels gently.
- Drain pasta, divide and place onto plates; ladle sauce over each portion and sprinkle remaining pine nuts and cheese on top. Serve at once.

STEAMED MUSSELS ORIENTAL STYLE

Serves 4

4 pounds mussels
3 teaspoons soy sauce
1½ tablespoons sesame oil
1½ tablespoons minced fresh ginger
⅓ cup rice vinegar
⅔ cup rice wine, vermouth, or sherry
1½ cups green onions, including tops, thinly sliced
4 garlic cloves, minced

- Scrub mussels and debeard them.
- Combine all ingredients in large pan and cook over medium-high heat until mussels open, 7 to 10 minutes. Discard any mussels which fail to open.
- Ladle into serving bowls along with the liquid.

Serve with rice to keep the oriental feeling or choose a crusty bread.

OVEN-FRIED OYSTERS

Serves 4

2   *10-ounce jars small Pacific oysters*
1¼   *cup biscuit mix*
5   *tablespoons yellow cornmeal*
½   *teaspoon garlic salt*
½   *teaspoon paprika*
¼   *teaspoon pepper*
2   *eggs*
½   *cup butter or margarine, melted*
2   *tablespoons chopped parsley*
    lemon wedges

- Drain oysters, pat dry and set aside.
- In a shallow bowl combine biscuit mix, cornmeal, garlic salt, paprika and pepper. In another shallow bowl, lightly beat eggs. Dip each oyster in egg, then in crumb mixture, and roll in melted margarine or butter to coat well. Place oysters in a single layer in oiled baking pan.
- Put pan in oven and bake uncovered, for 15 to 20 minutes at 425 degrees or until oysters are crisp and browned. Transfer to serving dish and sprinkle with parsley. Serve with lemon wedges.

Don't crowd the oysters as they bake so that they will be crisp. Egg whites may be used rather than whole eggs.

THYME-SCENTED STEAMED CLAMS

Serves 3 to 4

¾   *cup long grain white rice*
2   *tablespoons olive oil or salad oil*
1   *large onion, chopped*
2   *garlic cloves, minced*
1   *bay leaf*
½   *teaspoon thyme leaves*
3   *tablespoons chopped parsley*
1   *cup dry white wine or regular strength chicken broth*
1   *8-ounce bottle clam juice or chicken or fish broth*
2   *pounds small live hard-shell clams, well scrubbed, about 20 to 30 clams*
2   *tomatoes, seeded and chopped*

- Cook rice according to package directions and set aside.
- Heat oil in a 5 to 6-quart kettle. Add onion and garlic and cook, stirring, until onion is soft. Stir in bay leaf, thyme, parsley, wine or broth and clam juice. Cover, reduce heat and simmer for 5 minutes.
- Add clams; cover and simmer until clams open, about 10 to 12 minutes. Discard any which fail to open. Stir in tomatoes and rice; cover and cook until heated through. Ladle servings into individual bowls.

Green salad and crusty bread or rolls complete this meal very nicely.

GRAINS
&
PASTA
&
SIDES

CORN RISOTTO

Serves 4

3 cups fresh corn kernels (about 4 ears) or frozen corn, divided

¼ cup butter or margarine

3 tablespoons chopped shallots

½ cup Arborio rice or medium grain rice

¼ cup dry white wine

3 cups chicken stock or canned broth

⅓ cup freshly grated Parmesan cheese

¼ cup (or more) chicken broth
  salt and pepper to taste

- Purée 2 cups corn kernels in blender. Set aside.
- Heat butter or margarine in medium saucepan over medium heat. Add chopped shallots and sauté until translucent, about 5 minutes. Mix in rice and cook 1 minute, stirring constantly.
- Add wine and cook until all liquid is absorbed. Add 3 cups chicken stock and cook 10 minutes, stirring occasionally. Increase heat and boil until rice is thick and creamy, about 10 minutes, stirring occasionally.
- Add corn purée, 1 cup corn kernels and Parmesan cheese. Cook about 3 minutes longer. Thin with additional stock if necessary. Season with salt and pepper.

CIDER RICE PILAF

Serves 4

3 tablespoons butter

1 cup uncooked white or brown rice
  salt and pepper to taste

½ cup chopped onion

¾ cup chopped celery

1 teaspoon grated orange peel

¼ cup minced fresh parsley, divided

¼ teaspoon dried rosemary or ¾ teaspoon fresh

1¾ cups apple cider

- Heat butter in a skillet. Add rice and stir until golden. Add salt, pepper, onion, celery, and orange peel. Sauté 5 minutes more. Add half the parsley and all the rosemary.
- In a separate pan, bring the cider to a boil, then stir into the rice mixture. Cover the skillet and cook over low heat about ½ hour for white rice, or an hour for brown rice. Serve sprinkled with remaining parsley.

ORZO WITH LEMON PESTO

Serves 8

1 pound orzo
2 teaspoons salt
3 garlic cloves
2 cups tightly packed fresh basil
½ cup olive oil
½ cup lemon juice
½ cup freshly grated Parmesan cheese
  freshly grated black pepper to taste

- Cook orzo in boiling water with 1 teaspoon of the salt until al dente. Drain and refresh with cold water.
- In food processor, process the garlic and basil. Gradually add the olive oil, using only as much as is necessary to produce a thick sauce.
- Transfer basil mixture to a large mixing bowl. Add lemon juice and remaining teaspoon of salt. Combine orzo and basil mixture and stir in Parmesan cheese. Season with additional salt and pepper to taste. Chill for several hours.

GOLDEN COUSCOUS

Serves 6

½ cup currants
⅓ cup dry sherry
2 tablespoons unsalted butter
2 cups chicken stock
1 teaspoon cinnamon
1 teaspoon paprika
¼ teaspoon salt
1 cup couscous
½ cup finely diced carrots
4 green onions, thinly sliced, including tops
1 tablespoon fresh lime juice
⅓ cup toasted pine nuts
½ cup fresh orange juice
  salt and pepper to taste

- In small bowl, plump the currants in the sherry for 30 minutes. Drain, reserving the currants.
- In medium saucepan combine butter, stock, cinnamon, paprika and ¼ teaspoon salt and heat to boiling. Add couscous, stirring constantly. Cook until all of the liquid is absorbed, about 1 to 2 minutes.
- Remove from heat and add reserved currants. Cover, let stand for 10 to 15 minutes.
- Stir in carrots, onions, lime juice and pine nuts. Gradually add orange juice, a tablespoon at a time, until it is absorbed. Fluff couscous with a fork, season with salt and pepper and cover with foil. Heat in a 350 degree oven for 30 minutes.

GORGONZOLA POLENTA

Serves 6

3   cups milk
2   tablespoons unsalted butter
¾   cup cornmeal
⅓   cup freshly grated Parmesan cheese
½   cup crumbled Gorgonzola cheese
½   teaspoon salt
⅛   teaspoon freshly grated nutmeg

- In heavy saucepan, bring milk and butter to a boil. Gradually stir in cornmeal, whisking constantly, and bring back to a boil. Continue to stir constantly until mixture is very thick and smooth, about 5 minutes.
- Add cheeses, salt and nutmeg and beat until smooth.
- Butter 6 timbales or half-cup ramekins. Divide the mixture evenly, smoothing tops with spatula. Refrigerate 1 hour.
- Unmold on a well-buttered baking dish and bake at 450 degrees for 10 to 12 minutes. Place under broiler until lightly golden.

BARLEY PILAF

Serves 4 to 6

1   cup pearl barley
1   tablespoon butter or margarine
¼ to ½   cup pine nuts or slivered almonds
1   medium onion, chopped
¼   cup minced chives or green onions
½   cup minced fresh parsley
    salt and pepper to taste
2   cans (14 ounces each) beef or chicken broth
    fresh parsley for garnish

- Rinse barley and drain well.
- In skillet heat butter or margarine and lightly brown nuts. Remove from pan.
- Add onion, chives and barley to pan and brown lightly. Add minced parsley and salt and pepper. Blend broth into barley mixture. Pour into sprayed or buttered 1½-quart casserole.
- Bake, covered, at 350 degrees for 1½ hours until barley is tender. Garnish with parsley and nuts.

Optional additions: 1 cup sliced mushrooms, 1 teaspoon curry powder, and/or 1 cup pea pods. Add at the last minute.

SWEET AND SOUR LENTILS

Serves 4 to 6

1 cup lentils, rinsed and drained
2 cups water
2 beef bouillon cubes
1 bay leaf
1 teaspoon salt or to taste
¼ cup pineapple juice
¼ cup cider vinegar
¼ cup brown sugar
⅛ teaspoon ground cloves
1 garlic clove, minced
1 medium onion, sliced
1 green or red bell pepper, diced in large pieces

ᴥ Combine lentils, water, bouillon cubes and bay leaf in a large pot. Bring to a boil and simmer for 20 minutes.

ᴥ Add remaining ingredients, heat thoroughly and serve.

Serve over rice for a light entrée.

ORIENTAL COLD NOODLES

Serves 4

3½ tablespoons sesame oil
3½ tablespoons soy sauce
2½ tablespoons white rice vinegar
2 tablespoons sugar
2 teaspoons salt or to taste
1 to 2 teaspoons hot pepper oil or to taste
1 16-ounce package angel hair pasta
4 green onions including tops, chopped
2 tablespoons toasted sesame seeds

ᴥ Mix first 6 ingredients and set aside.

ᴥ Cook noodles until just tender. Drain and cool.

ᴥ Combine sauce with noodles and refrigerate for several hours.

ᴥ Before serving add green onions and toasted sesame seeds.

PASTA ROMA

Serves 4 to 6

 ½ pound mild Italian sausage sliced on the diagonal
 1 tablespoon olive oil
 ½ cup chopped onion
1 to 2 garlic cloves, crushed
 3 cups linguine
 2 tablespoons butter or margarine
 2 tablespoons flour
 1 cup milk, heated
 ½ cup sliced green onions
 ½ pound sliced mushrooms
 ¾ cup shredded mozzarella cheese
 2 tablespoons chopped fresh basil
 2 teaspoons chopped fresh oregano
 ¼ teaspoon chopped fresh sage
 ¼ teaspoon chopped fresh rosemary
 ½ cup sliced black olives
 1 cup diced tomatoes
 1 cup diced zucchini
 ½ cup freshly grated Parmesan cheese
 ¼ cup chopped fresh parsley

- Sauté sausage in olive oil and pour off fat. Add chopped onion and garlic; cook briefly and set aside.

- Cook linguine according to package directions and drain.

- Heat butter or margarine, add flour and cook to a foam; add hot milk and whisk until smooth. When slightly thickened, add onions, mushrooms, mozzarella cheese, seasonings, black olives, tomatoes, zucchini and sausage; toss lightly with cooked and drained linguine.

- Pour into a 2-quart non-metallic baking dish and bake, covered, at 375 degrees for 50 minutes.

- Remove lid, sprinkle with Parmesan, and cook 10 more minutes.

- Sprinkle with parsley and serve.

PASTA, SAGE, ROSEMARY AND THYME

Serves 4 to 6

3   garlic cloves
1   tablespoon fresh rosemary or 1½ teaspoons dried
     rosemary
1½   teaspoons fresh thyme or 1 teaspoon dried thyme
¼   teaspoon fresh sage or ⅛ teaspoon dried sage
1 to 2   small dried red chili peppers
¼   cup olive oil
4   cups chopped and seeded tomatoes or 28-ounce
     can whole plum tomatoes, drained
     salt and pepper to taste
1   pound spaghetti or vermicelli, cooked and drained
1   cup freshly grated Parmesan

- In a saucepan, sauté the garlic, rosemary, thyme, sage and chilies in the olive oil over medium heat for 2 to 3 minutes.
- Add tomatoes and cook over medium heat for 15 to 20 minutes until the sauce thickens slightly. Add salt and pepper to taste.
- Place hot pasta in a serving bowl. Strain the sauce over the pasta, pushing with a large spoon to extract all liquid. Sauce will be thin.
- Immediately toss the pasta with the cheese. Pass additional cheese.

PASTA WITH TOMATO AND PESTO SAUCE

Serves 4

Tomato Sauce

1   medium onion, chopped

2   small garlic cloves, minced

1   tablespoon olive oil

8   ripe Roma tomatoes or larger tomatoes, skinned and chopped (about 2½ cups)
    salt and pepper to taste

Pesto Sauce

1½   cups fresh basil leaves, stems removed

1½   cups fresh parsley, stems removed - can be part curly and part fresh cilantro

3   garlic cloves, minced

3   tablespoons pine nuts
    salt and pepper to taste

¾   cup extra virgin olive oil

½   cup freshly grated Parmesan cheese

½   cup freshly grated Romano cheese

Pasta

1   pound good quality pasta (A good brand is made with hard semolina durum wheat), cooked

⅓   cup grated Parmesan or Romano cheese

Tomato Sauce

➸ Sauté onions and garlic in oil until limp. Add tomatoes and cook until they are just soft. Add salt and pepper. Keep warm.

Pesto Sauce

➸ Put basil and parsley leaves, garlic, pine nuts, salt and pepper in large bowl of food processor. Process briefly, scrape sides. Add oil in a steady stream while processing, until just blended. Transfer to bowl and stir in cheeses.

Pasta

➸ Add ⅓ cup grated cheese and 2 tablespoons hot water to pasta; stir. Add pesto and tomato sauces, tossing lightly. Keep pasta warm. Serve with additional grated cheese.

When in Rome, it is polite to begin eating as soon as you are served your hot pasta.

NEAPOLITAN LASAGNA

Serves 12 as a side dish

2 tablespoons chopped onion

1 to 2 garlic cloves, minced

2 tablespoons olive oil

1 2 lb. 3 oz.-can plum tomatoes

3 tablespoons tomato paste

½ bay leaf

2 cloves

2 teaspoons fresh basil (½ teaspoon dried)

2 teaspoons fresh oregano (½ teaspoon dried)

¼ teaspoon pepper

1 16-ounce package spinach lasagna

1 16-ounce carton cottage cheese

1 package frozen spinach, thawed and squeezed dry

2 eggs

½ cup freshly grated Parmesan cheese

¼ teaspoon freshly grated nutmeg

⅛ teaspoon freshly ground pepper

¼ pound low-fat mozzarella, grated

2 tablespoons freshly grated Parmesan cheese

- Sauce: Sauté onion and garlic in olive oil until tender, stir in tomatoes, tomato paste, bay leaf, cloves, herbs, and pepper. Simmer 30 minutes, stirring occasionally. Remove bay leaf and cloves.
- While sauce is simmering, cook lasagna noodles according to package directions.
- Blend cottage cheese, drained spinach, eggs, Parmesan, nutmeg and pepper.
- Spread ⅓ of the sauce in a 9x13 baking dish. Lay ⅓ of the cooked noodles in a single layer on top of sauce. Spread with sauce, spoon on ½ of spinach mixture and sprinkle with ⅓ of the grated mozzarella cheese. Repeat layers, cover with remaining sauce. Sprinkle with mozzarella and Parmesan cheeses. Cover loosely with foil. Bake at 350 degrees for 40 minutes.

STUFFED SHELLS

Serves 6

1   15-ounce carton low-fat ricotta cheese
⅔   cup drained 2% small curd cottage cheese
1   cup shredded low-fat mozzarella cheese
¾   cup freshly grated Parmesan cheese
2   eggs
1   teaspoon or more crumbled oregano
      salt and pepper to taste
1   6-ounce can black olives, coarsely chopped
1   16-ounce package shells
3   cups spaghetti sauce

- Place first 7 ingredients in food processor and pulse briefly until mixed. Fold in olives.
- In a large pot with lots of water cook shells until just done. Drain. Stuff shells with cheese mixture.
- Put 1½ cups spaghetti sauce on bottom of 9x13-inch baking dish. Place filled shells on top. Cover with rest of sauce, garnish with a bit more crumbled oregano and Parmesan cheese.
- Bake at 350 degrees for about 20 minutes until bubbly.

Can be done the day before. Cover well with plastic wrap and refrigerate.

FETTUCCINE CAMBOZOLA

Serves 3 to 4

1   8-ounce package fresh fettuccine
1   8-ounce package frozen peas, defrosted
1   cup, about 6 ounces, diced cambozola or
      gorgonzola cheese
2   tablespoons hot water from cooked pasta
      fresh ground pepper

- Cook fettuccine as per recipe on package, about 3 minutes. Drain and reserve 2 tablespoons liquid. Return to pan. Stir in defrosted peas. Add cheese and the hot water. Gently mix over low heat until cheese melts and coats pasta, about 2 or 3 minutes.
- Lift onto warm dinner plates. Add pepper to taste.

CRISPY BAKED EGGPLANT WITH BLUE CHEESE SAUCE *Serves 4 to 5*

1 large eggplant, about 1½ pounds
2 eggs, or 4 egg whites
2 tablespoons milk
1 cup wheat germ
1 teaspoon basil
1 teaspoon dill
¼ teaspoon thyme
  Blue Cheese Sauce
  paprika
  minced parsley

Blue Cheese Sauce

1½ cups minced onion
2 garlic cloves, crushed or minced
3 tablespoons butter or margarine
½ teaspoon salt
¾ pound mushrooms, sliced
2 tablespoons fresh lemon juice
1 tablespoon whole wheat flour
1½ cups yogurt
¾ cup crumbled blue cheese
  black pepper to taste
½ teaspoon dill

◦ Slice eggplant very thin, no more than ¼ inch.

◦ Beat eggs with milk in 1 bowl; combine the wheat germ and herbs in another.

◦ Dip eggplant slices in liquid, then dredge in wheat germ.

◦ Bake on an oiled pan for 20 to 30 minutes, until the eggplant is crisp on the outside and tender on the inside (test with a fork).

◦ To serve, place several slices of eggplant on each plate and spoon Blue Cheese Sauce on top. Sprinkle with paprika and minced parsley.

Blue Cheese Sauce

◦ In a large heavy skillet, cook the onions and garlic in butter or margarine with salt until the onions are limp.

◦ Add mushrooms, lemon juice and flour; cook, stirring, over medium heat 5 to 8 minutes.

◦ Add remaining ingredients, lower heat, and stir. Cover and simmer 10 more minutes, stirring occasionally.

This could also be used as a meatless entrée.

BRONCO BEANS

Serves 8 to 10

2   15¼-ounce cans dark red kidney beans
1   15-ounce can black beans
1   15-ounce can white kidney beans
1   28-ounce can Italian plum tomatoes, drained and chopped
1   cup chopped onion
2 to 4   large garlic cloves, minced
⅓   cup dark molasses
¼   cup cider vinegar
2   tablespoons honey
2   teaspoons dried oregano
2   teaspoons dry mustard
2   teaspoons ground cumin
1½   teaspoons ground ginger
1½   teaspoons chili powder

• Rinse and drain beans. Place in an oven-proof casserole. Add remaining ingredients, folding together gently so beans don't break up.

• Bake, covered, at 350 degrees for 45 minutes. Remove cover, stir and bake, uncovered, 30 minutes more or until hot and bubbly.

Beans with a Zip!

SALSAS
&
CHUTNEYS
&
PRESERVES

PINEAPPLE SALSA

Makes About 2 Cups

1   20-ounce can crushed pineapple
1   teaspoon grated lime peel
½   cup minced red bell pepper
½   cup minced green bell pepper
1   tablespoon chopped green onion
2   teaspoons chopped fresh cilantro
2   teaspoons chopped green chilies or jalapeño chilies
     (optional)

- Drain ½ cup juice from the pineapple. Reserve for other uses.
- Combine all ingredients.

An excellent accompaniment to chicken or fish!

AVOCADO CORN SALSA

Makes 2⅓ Cups

1   cup fresh corn kernels or frozen, thawed
¼   cup chopped red bell pepper
¼   cup chopped yellow bell pepper
¼   cup diced tomatoes
2   tablespoons chopped fresh cilantro
2   tablespoons fresh lemon juice
1   tablespoon finely chopped shallots
½   jalapeño chili, minced
1   cup diced peeled avocado
     salt and pepper

- Cook corn in large pot of boiling water until just tender. Drain and cool completely. Transfer to medium bowl.
- Add remaining ingredients except avocado and toss gently. (Can be prepared 8 hours ahead. Cover and refrigerate.)
- Mix diced avocado into salsa. Season to taste with salt and pepper.

PAPAYA AND BLACK BEAN SALSA

Makes 4 Cups

  1 *ripe papaya or mango, peeled, seeded and finely diced*
  1 *15½-ounce can black beans, drained and rinsed*
  ½ *cup chopped red onion*
  ⅓ *cup orange juice*
  ¼ *cup lime juice*
  ⅓ *cup chopped fresh cilantro*
  1 *tablespoon ground cumin*
  1 *tablespoon minced chili pepper*
    salt and pepper to taste

➲ Mix all ingredients well. Chill for at least 2 hours.

Great with fish or in place of a summer salad.

MANGO PEACH CHUTNEY

5 Pints

1½ *cups sugar*
1½ *cups white vinegar*
  1 *large onion, chopped*
  1 *green pepper, seeded and diced*
  1 *clove garlic, minced or pressed*
  1 *lime, seeded and thinly sliced*
1½ *teaspoons ground cinnamon*
  ½ *teaspoon ground cloves*
  ½ *teaspoon ground allspice*
  1 *teaspoon salt*
⅛-¼ *teaspoon cayenne*
  ½ *cup raisins*
  3 *large ripe mangoes (about 2½ pounds total)*
  2 *pounds peaches or nectarines*

➲ Combine sugar, vinegar, onion, pepper, garlic, lime, cinnamon, cloves, allspice, salt, cayenne and raisins in a heavy 4 to 5 quart pot. Bring mixture to a boil; reduce heat and simmer, uncovered, stirring often to prevent sticking, about 1 hour or until thickened.

➲ Peel, pit and slice mangoes. Peel and slice peaches. Add mangoes and peaches to syrup and simmer, uncovered, stirring occasionally, about 30 minutes or until fruit is tender.

➲ Ladle chutney into hot pint canning jars, leaving ¼ inch head space. Attach lids. Process 10 minutes in a boiling water bath. Start counting time when the water returns to a boil.

APPLE GINGER CHUTNEY

Makes 3 Cups

2 large tart apples, peeled, cored and finely chopped
1 cup minced onion
½ cup cider vinegar
½ cup light brown sugar, packed
½ cup golden raisins
2 teaspoons peeled and minced fresh ginger root
½ cup minced red bell pepper
¼ teaspoon dry mustard
¼ teaspoon salt
¼ teaspoon hot pepper flakes, or to taste

- Mix all ingredients in non-corrosive pan. Bring to a boil and simmer until thickened, about 40 minutes, stirring frequently.
- Pour into sterilized jars, leaving ¼-inch head space. Seal and process at rolling boil in hot water bath for 10 minutes.

Good with rice dishes, pork, turkey, curries and cream cheese and crackers.

CRANBERRY CHUTNEY

Makes 2 Pints

1 pound cranberries, fresh or frozen, or 1 16-ounce can whole cranberry sauce
1 cup golden raisins
¾ cup sugar, or 1 cup for fresh berries
¼ teaspoon cinnamon
¼ teaspoon ground ginger
¼ teaspoon allspice
⅛ teaspoon ground cloves
⅔ cup cider vinegar
¼ cup slivered candied ginger, or to taste
¼ cup coarsely chopped slivered almonds

- Combine all ingredients except candied ginger and almonds. Simmer, uncovered, stirring occasionally, for 20 minutes or until mixture begins to thicken.
- Add candied ginger and almonds and stir to mix.
- Pour into sterilized jars, leaving ¼-inch head space. Seal and process at rolling boil in hot water bath for 10 minutes.

You don't have to wait for cranberry season to enjoy this chutney. Excellent with turkey, chicken, roast, scaloppini or on sandwiches. Good, too, with cream cheese on crackers!

RHUBARB CHUTNEY

Makes 2½ Pints

2   *pounds fresh rhubarb, rinsed and cut into 1-inch pieces*
2   *cups light brown sugar*
1½ *cups chopped white onion*
⅔   *cup cider vinegar*
⅓   *cup dried currants*
2   *teaspoons curry powder*
2   *teaspoons grated fresh ginger*
⅔   *teaspoon salt*

- Combine all ingredients in a non-corrosive pan. Cook over medium-low heat until boiling, stirring often. Reduce heat and cook, stirring often, until mixture is thickened, about 1 hour.
- Pour into sterilized jars, leaving ¼-inch head space. Seal and process at rolling boil in hot water bath for 10 minutes.

Good with poultry, pork, veal and rice dishes. Even less-than-enthusiastic rhubarb fans will enjoy this year round.

PLUM CHUTNEY

Makes 2½ Pints

1⅔ *cups cider vinegar, divided*
1   *white onion, finely chopped*
½   *teaspoon salt*
3   *cups granulated sugar*
1   *cup light brown sugar*
2   *large garlic cloves, crushed or chopped very fine*
½   *teaspoon allspice*
¼   *teaspoon cloves*
1   *teaspoon ground ginger*
4   *cups plums, washed and thinly sliced*
1   *cup golden raisins*
1   *6-ounce jar ginger marmalade or preserved ginger*

- Boil down 1⅓ cups vinegar with onion, salt, sugars, garlic and spices, until reduced to half. Add remaining vinegar and other ingredients. Simmer 1½ hours, stirring occasionally. If too much juice remains, remove fruit with slotted spoon. Boil down remaining liquid until it begins to thicken. Replace fruit, heat to boiling.
- Pour into sterilized jars, leaving ¼-inch head space. Seal and process at rolling boil in hot water bath for 10 minutes.

A rich flavor, good with beef, game or pork sandwiches, and rice dishes. Also good with cream cheese on crackers.

RED TOMATO CHUTNEY

Makes 2 Pints

1½ *pounds tomatoes*
½   *cup finely chopped white onion*
½   *teaspoon salt*
    pinch cayenne pepper
½   *teaspoon cardamom*
½   *teaspoon cinnamon*
½   *teaspoon allspice*
½   *teaspoon mace*
1   *teaspoon ground ginger*
1   *teaspoon paprika*
½   *cup brown sugar*
½   *cup malt vinegar*
½   *cup raisins*

- Skin tomatoes by plunging into boiling water for about 20 seconds. Skins will slip off easily. Quarter, remove seeds and coarsely chop.
- In a non-corrosive pan, simmer onion, salt and cayenne pepper, spices and tomatoes about 20 minutes, covered.
- Add sugar, vinegar and raisins. Cook, uncovered, stirring occasionally, about 1 hour or until chutney begins to thicken.
- Pour into sterilized jars, leaving ¼-inch head space. Seal and process at rolling boil in hot water bath for 10 minutes.

APRICOT AND ORANGE MARMALADE

2 *large oranges (or 3 small)*
4 *pounds apricots*
   sugar (quantity varies)

Makes 4 Pints

- Squeeze juice from the oranges; place in a large bowl. Remove inner membranes from orange peels and discard. Slice peels thinly and in a small pan cover with water and cook slowly until soft.

- Cut apricots into small pieces and drop into the orange juice. Stir to coat with juice to keep fruit from discoloring.

- Drain cooked peels; add to chopped apricots. Measure fruit and add ⅔ cup sugar for every cup of fruit. Use ¾ cup sugar if sweeter marmalade is desired.

- In a large kettle over high heat, cook marmalade at a rolling boil, stirring constantly. This will jell in 10 to 15 minutes if some of apricots are slightly green; otherwise it may take a little longer. Test a spoonful on a cold saucer if in doubt. The quicker it cooks the better the flavor.

- Pour into sterilized jars, leaving ¼-inch head space. Seal and process at rolling boil in hot water bath for 10 minutes.

RED HUCKLEBERRY MARMALADE

Makes 2 Pints

1   *large orange*
     water
4   *cups red huckleberries*
1   *cup tart, unsweetened applesauce*
3   *cups sugar, approximately*

- Squeeze juice from orange and reserve. Remove membranes from juiced shells and slice peel into small pieces. In a small saucepan, cook peel until tender in water to barely cover, about 15 to 20 minutes. Drain.

- Combine cooked peel with huckleberries, applesauce and orange juice. Measure fruit mixture into large non-corrosive pot. Add ¾ cup sugar to every cup of fruit. Bring to a rolling boil over high heat, stirring constantly. Continue cooking at rolling boil, stirring constantly, until jelling point is reached, about 5 to 15 minutes. Test a spoonful on a cold saucer. Marmalade will look thick and shiny when done.

- Pour into sterilized jars, leaving ¼-inch head space. Seal and process at rolling boil in hot water bath for 10 minutes.

This is a lovely way to enjoy our native huckleberries all year. Oregon grape, both Mahonia nervosa and M. aquifolium, is another wonderful Northwest native fruit that ripens in the late summer after a beautiful display of masses of small bright yellow flowers in earliest spring. It can provide a unique and delicious taste treat with your Thanksgiving turkey. Use the juice from gently cooked, crushed and strained fruit in your favorite jelly recipe. If not enough fruit is available, apple juice can be added.

MICROWAVE ORANGE MARMALADE

Makes 1½ Cups

1   *large unblemished orange*
     equal amount of sugar, determined by amount of
     processed orange

- Cut orange, including peel, into chunks and chop coarsely in food processor. Measure amount of chopped orange, then add an equal amount of sugar.
- Mix orange and sugar well in microwaveable bowl and microwave 4 minutes, full power. Stir mixture and microwave 3 minutes. Check to see if marmalade is jelling; if thicker consistency is desired, microwave 1 more minute.
- Pour into sterilized jars, refrigerate and enjoy!

VERY BERRY JAM

Makes 3 Pints

1   *cup peeled and chopped tart apples, such as*
     Jonathans
1   *cup fresh orange juice*
1   *cup red raspberries*
1   *cup strawberries*
1   *cup red huckleberries*
1   *cup black Ribier grapes, seeded*
1   *cup sugar for each cup of mashed fruit*

- Cook apples in orange juice until soft; mash.
- In a large bowl combine remaining fruits; mash. Add apple-orange juice mixture and measure into large non-corrosive pan. Add sugar, 1 cup for each cup of mashed fruit. Bring to a rolling boil over high heat, stirring constantly, and cook about 5 to 15 minutes. Test a spoonful on a cold saucer; jam will look shiny and thick when done.
- Pour into sterilized jars, leaving ¼-inch head space. Seal and process at rolling boil in hot water bath for 5 minutes.

RHUBARB CONSERVE

Makes 3 Pints

2   pounds rhubarb
¼   cup water
      juice of 1 lemon
2½ to 3 cups sugar
1   tablespoon grated ginger root
1   cup golden raisins
      grated rind of 1 lemon
      grated rind of 1 orange
½   cup chopped slivered almonds

☙ Cut rhubarb into 1-inch chunks; add water and simmer gently until rhubarb is pulpy. Add lemon juice, sugar, ginger and raisins. Stir while boiling until thick. Add lemon and orange rind and almonds near end of cooking time to retain texture.

☙ Pour into sterilized jars, leaving ¼-inch head space. Seal and process at rolling boil in hot water bath for 10 minutes.

Good as an unusual jam on scones or English muffins. A tasty way to enjoy rhubarb flavor year round.

APPLE PUMPKIN BUTTER

Makes 2 Pints

4   cups apple cider
4   cups cored, peeled and thinly sliced apples
1   cup sugar
1   cup cooked pumpkin, fresh or canned
½   teaspoon cinnamon

☙ Boil cider until it is reduced to 2 cups. Add sliced apples and cook slowly until mixture begins to thicken, stirring and mashing the apple slices.

☙ Add sugar, pumpkin and cinnamon. Continue cooking and stirring until a little dropped on a cool plate is of good spreading consistency.

☙ Pour into sterilized jars, leaving ¼-inch head space. Seal and process at rolling boil in hot water bath for 10 minutes.

VEGETABLES

"SEASON TO TASTE"

The flavor of fresh vegetables can be enhanced in many ways. Here are some of our favorites for you to try. Start with small amounts of seasonings, taste, and add more if you like.

Acorn squash: Fill cavity with applesauce or brown sugar or fresh or frozen blueberries.

Asparagus: Slice diagonally in 2-inch pieces, stir-fry with garlic and soy.
Curry mayonnaise
Cold with raspberry vinegar
Soft buttered bread crumbs, and/or crumbled hard boiled egg

Beets: Frozen orange juice concentrate
Sour cream
Brown sugar and lemon juice
Puree with cooked apples and a dash of raspberry vinegar.

Broccoli: Equal parts yogurt and mayonnaise, Dijon mustard to taste
Cream cheese thinned with a little milk
Marjoram or dill or garlic butter

Brussels Sprouts: Cook in equal parts water and rice wine vinegar and 1 teaspoon sugar. Drain and sprinkle with ¾ teaspoon sugar, shake over high heat to glaze.
Red Tokay grapes added just before serving
Equal parts grated Parmesan cheese and dry bread crumbs

Cabbage: Dill and mayonnaise
Cream cheese and celery seeds
Sour cream and caraway seeds

Carrots: Cook in fresh orange juice, add honey.
Dill
Mustard, touch of honey or brown sugar
Orange marmalade
Crushed pineapple and dill

Cauliflower: Cheese sauce
Chopped chives

Corn:	Steam, season butter with chili powder or oregano.
Green Beans:	Picanté sauce, crumbled crisp bacon, chopped celery or jicama Snipped fresh basil Tarragon and lemon juice
Napa Cabbage:	Steam with sliced onions, frozen peas.
Parsnips:	Cook in a small amount of canned pear juice. Caraway seed
Peas:	Mint leaves and finely chopped green onion Small amount mint jelly Dash sugar and chervil Fresh mushrooms
Peppers:	Stir-fry green, red, yellow, and orange pepper slices.
Potatoes:	New potatoes with dill and 1 tablespoon minced fresh mint or use 1 teaspoon balsamic vinegar and dill.
Rutabagas:	Mash with equal parts potatoes. Peel and sauté with peeled pumpkin, sprinkle with nutmeg.
Spinach:	Toasted sesame seeds Cream cheese Rice wine vinegar
Tomatoes:	Stuff with bread crumbs and herbs or herbed rice or peas or seasoned corn. Add to zucchini, yellow summer squash or green beans along with sliced onion, sliced peppers. Broil or bake at 400 degrees with one of the following toppings: bread crumbs, fresh basil, dash Worcestershire sauce, grated cheese.
Turnips:	Dijon mustard, lemon juice Raw with dips
Zucchini:	Stir-fried strips with fine herbs or garlic or onion Dill Parmesan cheese Cooked, cut lengthwise, hollowed out and filled with bread crumbs and herbs or seasoned rice or mushrooms and cheese

GREEK SPANAKOPITA

Serves 9 to 10

1   package filo dough

¼   pound butter, melted

1   medium yellow onion, chopped

2   tablespoons olive oil

4   tablespoons fresh dill, chopped (or 2 tablespoons dry)

10   green onions, chopped

½   cup fresh parsley

2   10-ounce packages frozen chopped spinach, cooked and drained

     salt and pepper to taste

3   eggs

½   pound feta cheese

1   pound small curd cottage cheese

½   pound grated Parmesan cheese

❧ Unroll filo dough onto flat surface. Cover stack with a slightly damp towel. Remove 1 sheet of filo dough and put it in a 9x13-inch oiled baking dish allowing it to come up the sides and ends. Using a pastry brush, brush sparingly with melted butter. Top with a second sheet. Brush with butter. Continue layering and buttering until ten sheets are used. Set aside.

❧ Sauté chopped yellow onion in olive oil until soft. Add dill, green onions and parsley. Cook for 5 minutes. Add cooked drained spinach. Stir well and cool.

❧ Beat eggs. Add feta cheese, cottage cheese and Parmesan cheese, then add the onion-spinach mixture. Spread mixture on filo dough. Cut ten sheets of filo to fit baking dish. Place first sheet on the spinach filling; brush with butter. Continue layering and buttering.

❧ Using a sharp knife, cut through the filo, making serving-size pieces. Bake at 350 degrees for 50 minutes, or until crust is golden brown.

Makes a wonderful cold leftover!

MALAYSIAN ACHAR

Serves 6 to 8

½   *English or thin skinned cucumber*
3   *large carrots*
3   *cups cauliflowerets*
½   *cup sesame seeds*
⅓   *cup salad oil*
2   *cloves garlic, minced or pressed*
½   *cup minced shallots*
½   *cup distilled white vinegar*
¼   *cup sugar*
     soy sauce
     arugula leaves for garnish (optional)

- Slice cucumber and carrots into 4-inch long slivers. Break cauliflower into smaller flowerets. Set vegetables aside.
- Place frying pan or wok over medium heat. Add sesame seeds and stir until golden brown, 2 to 3 minutes. Remove from pan and set aside.
- Pour oil into pan. When hot, add garlic and shallots and cook until shallots are soft. Increase heat to high and add vinegar, sugar, cauliflower, and carrots. Stir fry until vegetables are tender-crisp. Add cucumber and heat through. If desired, season slightly with soy sauce.
- Transfer to a serving plate and sprinkle with sesame seeds. Garnish with arugula.
- Serve warm or at room temperature.

This colorful medley of sweet and sour vegetables is a good choice with any spicy entree.

MUSHROOMS AU GRATIN

Serves 4

1 pound fresh mushrooms, sliced
2 tablespoons butter
⅓ cup sour cream
 dash pepper
1 tablespoon flour
¼ cup chopped fresh parsley
½ cup shredded Swiss cheese

- Sauté mushrooms in butter until lightly browned. Cover pan for about 2 minutes and cook until mushrooms exude juices.
- Blend sour cream with pepper and flour. Stir into mushrooms until blended and beginning to boil. Pour into a 9-inch pie pan and sprinkle with parsley and cheese.
- Bake at 425 degrees for about 10 minutes.

Make this up ahead of time and refrigerate. Bake at the last minute; be sure to increase the baking time accordingly. Also a delicious filling for crepes!

TRI-COLORED VEGETABLE TART

Serves 12

1½ pounds Idaho russet potatoes, skins left on and thinly sliced
4 tablespoons olive oil, divided
 salt and pepper to taste
1 pound zucchini or yellow summer squash, thinly sliced
3 ripe tomatoes, sliced
3 cloves garlic, chopped
½ teaspoon Italian herbs
½ cup chopped fresh parsley

- Spread potato slices evenly on bottom of lightly greased 9x13-inch baking dish. Drizzle 1 tablespoon oil over potatoes; season with salt and pepper.
- Spread squash slices on top of potatoes; top with slices of tomato. Add garlic, herbs and parsley to remaining olive oil and pour over vegetables.
- Bake at 375 degrees for 50 to 60 minutes or until vegetables are tender.

Optional vegetable additions: rings of green pepper and onion slices.

PUMPKIN AND APPLE CASSEROLE

Serves 4 to 6

2   medium sweet apples such as Golden Delicious,
    peeled, cored and chopped
1   medium onion, chopped
½   cup diced carrots
½   cup diced celery
3   cloves garlic, pressed
1   bay leaf
1   teaspoon dry thyme leaves
1   teaspoon dry basil leaves
1   tablespoon butter
½   cup chicken broth
1   can (1 lb.) solid packed pumpkin or 2 cups cooked
    and mashed squash such as Hubbard or banana.
    salt and pepper to taste

⋅ Combine all ingredients except pumpkin or squash in a frying pan over high heat. Stir often until liquid has evaporated and vegetables are tender, about 20 minutes. Discard bay leaf. Stir pumpkin into the apple-vegetable mixture. Spread in a 1½-quart casserole.

⋅ Bake, uncovered, at 400 degrees for 25 minutes.

Just right for Thanksgiving.

POTATOES PATATINI

Serves 6

2   teaspoons olive oil
1   large onion, halved and thinly sliced
1 to 2   garlic cloves, minced
3   large white potatoes, peeled and thinly sliced
¼   teaspoon dried thyme, crushed
¼   teaspoon salt
    freshly ground black pepper
1   cup chicken broth
2   tablespoons grated Parmesan cheese

⋅ In a non-stick skillet heat the olive oil over medium heat. Add the onion and garlic and sauté until soft, about 5 to 10 minutes.

⋅ Place half of the potatoes in a 9x13-inch baking dish; cover with onions. Sprinkle with thyme, salt and pepper. Cover with the remaining potatoes. Pour the broth over all and sprinkle with Parmesan cheese.

⋅ Bake at 425 degrees for 40 minutes or until tender. Let cool a few minutes before serving.

A much lighter scalloped potato recipe than the usual.

NEW POTATOES BAKED WITH BAY LEAVES AND LEMON

Serves 6

¼ cup plus 2 tablespoons fresh lemon juice
1½ teaspoons dried oregano, crumbled
 1 teaspoon grated lemon peel
 1 teaspoon salt
¼ teaspoon freshly ground pepper
½ cup olive oil
 2 pounds new red potatoes, quartered
20 small bay leaves

- Mix lemon juice, oregano, lemon peel, salt and pepper in bowl. Whisk in oil. Add potatoes and toss well. Transfer to a lightly oiled shallow 2-quart baking dish. Tuck bay leaves around potatoes.
- Bake at 375 degrees, turning potatoes about every ten minutes while they cook, and bake until potatoes are golden brown and a knife pierces the center easily, about 40 minutes. Discard bay leaves.

YAM OR SWEET POTATO BAKE

Serves 6 to 8

 4 large yams or sweet potatoes
 2 eggs, beaten (optional)
 2 tablespoons grated onion
½ teaspoon salt
⅛ teaspoon grated nutmeg
     dash cinnamon
⅛ teaspoon allspice
¼ cup melted butter
⅓ cup lemon juice

- Scrub and bake yams in a 350 degree oven until well done, approximately 1 to 1½ hours.
- Peel yams and whip in large bowl of mixer. Add remaining ingredients. Spread in a buttered 3-quart baking dish.
- Bake at 375 degrees for 20 minutes.

A variation of this recipe uses orange juice instead of lemon juice and is topped with toasted pecan halves.

TWO POTATO PURÉE

Serves 6

3   medium potatoes, peeled and cut into 1½-inch
     chunks
2   medium sweet potatoes, peeled and cut into 1½-
     inch chunks
4   medium carrots, sliced 1½-inch thick
3   large garlic cloves, peeled and cut in half
1   teaspoon cumin
½   teaspoon curry powder (optional)
½   teaspoon salt
½   teaspoon freshly ground pepper
     dash cayenne pepper
1   cup water
2   tablespoons margarine or butter
     fresh parsley

- Simmer all ingredients except margarine and parsley in water for about 20 minutes until tender. Drain, saving water. Puree vegetables in food processor, adding cooking water until the proper consistency is reached. Add parsley and margarine.
- Serve at once or hold in a 200 degree oven in a covered baking dish.

MINT-GLAZED POTATOES

Serves 4

12 to 16 small unpeeled round red potatoes
1   tablespoon margarine
1   tablespoon sugar
1   tablespoon minced fresh mint
1   teaspoon balsamic vinegar

- Put potatoes in vegetable steamer over boiling water. Steam 20 minutes or until tender. Place in a bowl.
- Heat margarine over medium heat; add sugar. Cook 1 minute, stirring. Remove from heat, add mint and vinegar and stir. Pour over the hot potatoes, stirring gently to coat.

BAKED SHERRY CARROTS

Serves 4

3   *cups grated carrots, approximately 1 bunch*
2   *tablespoons melted margarine*
1   *tablespoon lemon juice*
2   *tablespoons dry sherry*
½   *teaspoon salt*
1   *tablespoon chopped chives or green onions*

- Place grated carrots in a casserole dish. Drizzle margarine, lemon juice, and sherry over carrots. Sprinkle with salt and chives.
- Bake at 350 degrees for 30 minutes.

This dish retains a fresh garden crispness, texture and flavor.

BROILED TOMATOES WITH DILL SAUCE

Serves 8

½   *cup sour cream*
¼   *cup mayonnaise*
2   *tablespoons finely chopped onion*
1   *teaspoon snipped fresh dill or ¼ teaspoon dried dill*
4   *large firm ripe tomatoes*
    salt and pepper to taste
    butter or margarine

- Combine sour cream, mayonnaise, onion and dill; mix well. Chill.
- Core tomatoes and cut in half crosswise. Season cut surfaces with salt and pepper, dot with a little bit of butter or margarine. Broil, cut side up, 3 inches from heat, about 5 minutes.
- Serve immediately with the dill sauce spooned over the hot tomatoes.

BROILED VEGETABLE KABOBS

Serves 6 to 8

1   *medium green pepper*
1   *medium yellow summer squash*
1   *medium zucchini squash*
1   *medium onion*
8   *large mushrooms*
8   *cherry tomatoes (or chunks of large tomatoes)*
    melted butter or oil and vinegar salad dressing
8   *skewers*

- Cut pepper and squash into 1-inch chunks. Cut onion into quarters and separate.
- Thread all vegetables on skewers beginning with the mushrooms and ending with the cherry tomatoes. Brush with butter or salad dressing.
- Grill kabobs over medium coals 10 to 12 minutes, turning occasionally for even cooking.

To accompany barbecued meat or fish.

BURMESE CURRIED MUSHROOMS

Serves 6 to 8

2   *pounds large mushrooms*
1   *cup chopped onion*
2   *garlic cloves, minced*
1   *teaspoon turmeric*
1½ *teaspoons salt*
¼   *teaspoon dried ground chili pepper (optional)*
3   *tablespoons oil*
1   *onion, thinly sliced*
2   *tablespoons lime or lemon juice*

- Wash, drain and quarter mushrooms.
- Process chopped onion, garlic, turmeric, salt and chili pepper in food processor until mixture forms a paste.
- Heat oil in skillet; add spice mixture, mushrooms and sliced onions. Sauté for 10 minutes, stirring frequently. Sprinkle with lime juice.

Also makes a great starter!

MANDALAY CUCUMBERS

Serves 6

4 cucumbers, peeled
6 tablespoons vinegar, divided
1 teaspoon salt
½ cup oil
4 onions, thinly sliced
4 garlic cloves, sliced
1 teaspoon turmeric
1 teaspoon sugar
½ teaspoon freshly ground black pepper

- Cut cucumbers in half lengthwise; remove seeds and cut crosswise in ½-inch pieces.
- Cover cucumbers with hot water; add 3 tablespoons vinegar and bring to a boil. Cook until transparent. Drain and sprinkle with salt; set aside.
- Heat oil in skillet; sauté onions and garlic until browned. Remove onions and garlic from pan.
- Stir turmeric, sugar, pepper and 3 tablespoons vinegar into oil and pour over cucumbers.
- Add onions and garlic; toss and cool.

More flavorful when prepared ahead. Also very good as an starter.

BREADS

Sticky Buns

Serves 10 to 12

2   packages dry yeast
2   cups warm water, divided
4   tablespoons sugar, divided
2   teaspoons salt
2   tablespoons oil
1   small potato, boiled, peeled and mashed
4 to 5   cups unbleached white bread flour
1   cup whole wheat flour
6   tablespoons butter, softened
2½   cups dark brown sugar, divided
1   teaspoon cinnamon
½   cup chopped walnuts
1   cup heavy cream

- Dissolve yeast in ½ cup of water with 1 teaspoon of sugar and set aside.

- Combine remaining water and sugar, salt, oil, and potato in a large bowl. Add 1 cup of white flour and mix well.

- Add yeast mixture, whole wheat flour and enough of remaining flour to make a soft dough. Mix well. Knead, either by hand or with a heavy duty mixer dough hook, for 4 minutes. Place dough in a clean, buttered bowl and cover tightly with plastic wrap. Let rise in a warm place for about 1 hour or until doubled in size.

- Turn dough out and knead for an additional 4 minutes. Roll dough into a rectangle about 12 by 16 inches. Spread with butter and sprinkle on ½ cup brown sugar, cinnamon and nuts. Roll dough up lengthwise and cut into 1¼-inch slices.

- Butter a 9x13-inch baking dish and spread 2 cups of brown sugar on bottom. Arrange sliced rolls on top of sugar. Pour cream carefully around and between rolls—NOT ON THE ROLLS.

- Let rise in a warm place for about 1 hour or until the rolls are double in size. Bake at 375 degrees for 30 minutes. Let cool for 5 minutes and invert on foil. Serve warm.

Absolutely, positively, decadent! If you can't get an early start on these, make them the day before and reheat them in foil—it's worth it.

GUILT-FREE CINNAMON ROLLS

Serves 8 to 10

1   large Russet potato, peeled and cubed
1   envelope dry yeast
½   teaspoon sugar
½   cup warm water
½   cup skimmed evaporated milk
¼   cup honey
3   tablespoons vegetable oil
1   teaspoon salt
5   cups unbleached flour
1   egg white, beaten
1¼ cups light brown sugar
¾   cup raisins
2   teaspoons cinnamon

- Cook potato in boiling water until tender. Drain, reserving ¾ cup cooking liquid.

- Mash potato; measure 1 cup and transfer to large bowl. Mix ¾ cup cooking liquid into potato. Cool to lukewarm.

- Sprinkle yeast and sugar over ½ cup warm water in small bowl. Stir to dissolve. Let stand until foamy, about 10 minutes.

- Add yeast mixture, milk, honey, oil and salt to mashed potato mixture. Stir in 2 cups flour and beat with electric mixer three minutes on medium speed. Stir in enough remaining flour to make a soft dough.

- Knead about 5 minutes until smooth and elastic. Let rise in greased bowl about 45 minutes until doubled. Punch down.

- Roll out to a 20x15-inch rectangle. Brush dough lightly with egg white.

- Blend brown sugar, raisins and cinnamon together and spread evenly over dough leaving a 1-inch border on all sides.

- Start on long side and roll up tightly jelly-roll fashion; cut to desired size. Let rise until light, about 20 to 30 minutes, on a greased baking sheet.

- Bake at 350 degrees for 20 to 30 minutes depending on the size. When done, centers should spring back when lightly pressed.

REFECTORY RYE BREAD

2   packages dry yeast
1½   cups warm water
¼   cup molasses
⅓   cup honey
1   tablespoon salt
1   teaspoon grated orange rind
1   teaspoon ground fennel seed
2½   cups sifted, finely milled rye flour or 1 cup rye
       flour and 1½ cups whole wheat flour
2   tablespoons softened butter
2½ to 3   cups sifted all-purpose flour

- In a large bowl, crumble yeast into water. Add molasses, honey, salt, orange rind and fennel.
- Stir in rye flour and butter. Beat together until smooth.
- Add all-purpose flour. If the dough is soft to handle, use the larger amount of flour. Knead until smooth, elastic and satiny. Let rise until double, about 1½ hours.
- Punch down. Shape into 2 slightly flattened ovals on a greased baking sheet dusted with corn meal or 2 greased bread pans. Let rise until almost double, about 1 hour.
- Make four ¼-inch diagonal slashes in the top of the loaves. Bake at 375 degrees for 30 to 35 minutes.

A moist aromatic loaf that keeps well. Try this recipe with Arboretum Honey from our gift shop!

Bran Rolls

1   package dry yeast
½   cup warm water
½   cup boiling water
½   cup shortening
⅓   cup sugar
½   cup whole bran
¾   teaspoon salt
1   egg, beaten
3   cups sifted flour

- Sprinkle yeast on warm water; stir to dissolve.
- Pour boiling water over shortening in mixing bowl; stir in sugar, bran, and salt. Cool to lukewarm. Add beaten egg.
- Stir in yeast; add flour, ½ cup at a time.
- Cover and let rise in warm place until almost doubled, about 2½ hours. Punch down.
- Drop dough from spoon into greased muffin cups, filling cups half full. Cover and let rise until doubled, about 1 hour.
- Bake in 375 degree oven for 15 minutes.

No kneading or shaping is necessary!

PARTY BREAD STICKS

Makes 3 Dozen

3 to 3½ cups flour
    1 tablespoon sugar
    1 teaspoon salt
    2 packages dry yeast
    ¼ cup salad oil
  1¼ cups warm water
    1 egg white beaten with 1 tablespoon water
       coarse salt or poppy, sesame or other seeds

- In large bowl mix 2 cups flour, sugar, salt and yeast; add oil gradually. Stir in warm water and beat for 2 minutes. Add ½ cup more flour and beat again. Stir in remaining flour.
- Turn out onto well-floured board with floured hands; work into a small ball.
- Shape dough into an even log and cut into 2 equal pieces. Cut each log into eight pieces. Arrange about 1-inch apart on oiled baking sheets.
- Let rise for 15 minutes and paint with egg white and seeds or salt.
- Bake at 300 degrees for 25 to 30 minutes.

Try adding ½ cup grated Cheddar cheese, ¼ cup Parmesan cheese, a pinch of herb seasoning mix and ¼ teaspoon onion salt.

FEATHERWEIGHT FRIDGE ROLLS

Makes 4 Dozen

2   cups lukewarm water
½   cup sugar
1½ teaspoons salt
2   packages dry yeast
1   egg
¼   cup shortening
6½ to 7 cups flour

- Mix together water, sugar and salt. Add yeast and stir to dissolve. Add egg and shortening. Mix in 2 cups of flour with heavy duty mixer or food processor. Continue to add remaining flour until consistency is smooth.
- Place in greased bowl, cover with waxed paper and a damp towel, and refrigerate. Let rise 2 hours. Punch dough down. (Dough will keep up to 4 days in the refrigerator.)
- Shape into desired rolls and place in greased pans. Cover and let rise 2 hours at room temperature. Bake at 400 degrees for 12 to 15 minutes.

To make "Brown and Serve" rolls: Bake at 275 degrees for 20 to 30 minutes. Do not let brown. Remove from pans and cool at room temperature. Store in freezer bags or aluminum foil in freezer. To serve, brown rolls at 400 degrees for 7 to 10 minutes.

FLATBREAD

Serves 4 to 6

- 1   cup finely chopped nuts, or cracked wheat or wheat germ
- 2   cups flour
- 1   tablespoon sugar
- ½   teaspoon soda
- ¾   teaspoon salt
- ⅓   cup margarine
- ¾   cup buttermilk

- Blend all ingredients in food processor or mixer.
- Shape into individual rounds about the size of an egg and roll each one paper thin on well floured board.
- Bake on a greased cookie sheet at 400 degrees for about 10 minutes.

Great with salads or soups for added crunch!

IRISH SODA BREAD

Makes One Loaf

- 1   cup whole wheat or rye flour
- 1   cup all purpose flour
- 1   tablespoon sugar
- 1   teaspoon salt
- 1   teaspoon baking soda
- ⅓   cup cracked wheat
- 2   cups buttermilk or more

- Sift dry ingredients into a large mixing bowl. Make a well in the center and add the buttermilk. Mix until just blended.
- Turn the dough on to a flat floured board and knead lightly for a few minutes. Pat into a flattish round shape about 2 inches thick and cut a cross on the top to prevent cracking during baking. The cuts should go over the sides of the loaf.
- Brush with buttermilk and transfer the loaf carefully to a flat floured baking pan. Bake at 350 degrees for 35 minutes. When done the loaf should sound hollow when tapped on the underside.

Compliments of our Arboretum "First Lady".

PUMPKIN BREAD

Makes 2 Loaves

⅔ cup butter, softened
2⅔ cups sugar
4 eggs
2 cups canned pumpkin
⅔ cup eggnog, milk may be substituted
2½ cups flour
1 cup whole wheat flour
2 teaspoons baking soda
½ teaspoon baking powder
1 teaspoon salt
1 teaspoon cinnamon
½ teaspoon ground cloves
½ teaspoon ground cardamom
1 cup chopped pecans

- Cream together butter and sugar; beat in eggs; add pumpkin and eggnog, stirring until blended.
- Combine dry ingredients; add to pumpkin mixture and stir just until blended; fold in nuts.
- Spoon into 2 9x5-inch greased loaf pans and bake at 350 degrees for 1 hour or until done. Remove from pans when cool.

STRAWBERRY BREAD

Makes 2 Large or 4 Small Loaves

3 cups flour
1 teaspoon baking soda
1 teaspoon salt
1 teaspoon cinnamon
2 cups sugar
4 eggs, beaten
1¼ cups oil
2 cups strawberries, thawed
1¼ cups chopped nuts

- In a large bowl, combine all dry ingredients; stir to mix. Add eggs, oil, strawberries and nuts. Stir until all ingredients are moistened.
- Spoon into well-greased loaf pans, either 2 large or 4 smaller ones, and bake at 350 degrees for 60 to 70 minutes. Cool in pans for 5 minutes and remove to wire racks.

SPICY BANANA BREAD

Makes One Loaf

½   cup butter or margarine
1   cup sugar
2   eggs
2   cups flour
1   teaspoon baking soda
½   teaspoon salt
½   teaspoon cinnamon
¼   teaspoon nutmeg
¼   teaspoon cloves
1   cup mashed bananas
¼   cup orange juice
1   cup chopped walnuts
1   teaspoon vanilla

❧ Cream butter and sugar; gradually add eggs, one at a time.

❧ Combine dry ingredients and add, alternately, with mashed bananas and orange juice, stirring only to blend. Fold in nuts and vanilla.

❧ Pour batter into a greased 9x5x3-inch loaf pan and bake at 350 degrees for 1 hour or until a wooden pick comes out clean. Let cool 30 minutes in pan.

Three small pans are a good substitute. Watch the timing!

When using glass pans, reduce oven temperature by 25 degrees.

HOMESTEAD OATMEAL BREAD

Makes 2 Loaves

1   cup rolled oats
2   cups boiling water
1   yeast cake
½   cup lukewarm water
½   cup dark molasses
½   cup sugar
1½ teaspoons salt
1   tablespoon melted shortening
4½ cups sifted flour

- Combine rolled oats and boiling water. Let stand 1 hour.
- Soften yeast in lukewarm water; add to cooled oats with molasses, sugar, salt and melted shortening. Add flour and let rise for 1½ hours in warm place or until light.
- Beat down thoroughly. Place in 2 greased bread pans. Let rise again for 45 minutes.
- Bake at 400 degrees for 10 minutes. Reduce heat to 375 degrees and continue baking for 50 minutes. While still hot, rub top of bread with soft butter. Cool on racks.

Batter bread, no kneading required. This recipe dates all the way back to the 1860's!

To save time when making yeast breads, use the sponge method of mixing: mix yeast, sugar, liquid and 2 cups of flour. Mix thoroughly with mixer and let stand in warm location for 20 minutes. Beat down and add remaining ingredients. Knead for 6-8 minutes, either by hand, in food processor or with bread hook of a heavy mixer. Shape into desired shapes and place in greased baking pans. Let rise for 45 minutes.

BLUEBERRY CORN MUFFINS

Makes 7 to 8 Medium Muffins

1   cup flour
1   cup corn meal
4   tablespoons sugar
3   teaspoons baking powder
    pinch of salt
2   whole large eggs (or 3 eggs whites)
1   cup milk
4   tablespoons vegetable oil
½   teaspoon ground cinnamon
1   teaspoon grated orange or lemon rind
1   cup blueberries

- In medium mixing bowl, blend flour, corn meal, sugar, baking powder and salt.
- Make a well in center and add eggs, milk, oil, cinnamon and orange or lemon rind.
- Mix liquid ingredients together, slowly stirring in the dry ingredients. When well blended add blueberries.
- Spray muffin pan with non-stick coating and spoon batter into pan, filling each cup ⅔ full.
- Bake at 375 degrees for 20 to 30 minutes until golden brown.

THREE-LAYER CORN BREAD

Serves 4 to 6

1   cup coarse corn meal
½   cup whole wheat flour
½   cup unbleached white flour
2   teaspoons baking powder
½   teaspoon salt
1   egg
¼ to ½ cup honey or molasses
¼   cup oil
3   cups milk or buttermilk

- Combine dry ingredients. Blend remaining ingredients and stir into dry ingredients. Mixture will be quite watery.
- Pour into a greased 9-inch square pan and bake at 350 degrees for 50 minutes or until top is springy when gently touched.

This one batter makes three layers: the corn meal settles, a bran mixture rises to the top and in the middle is an egg-custardy layer. Easy! Glorious! Amazing!

CRUNCHY CHEESE AND ONION BREAD

Serves 8 to 10

1   *cup boiling water*
⅓   *cup Bulgur wheat*
1½ *cups all-purpose flour*
½   *cup yellow cornmeal*
2   *tablespoons grated Parmesan cheese*
2   *tablespoons sugar*
1   *tablespoon baking powder*
½   *teaspoon oregano*
     dash of black pepper
2   *eggs*
1   *cup milk*
¼   *cup olive oil*
1   *cup mild Cheddar cheese*
½   *cup sun-dried tomatoes in oil, drained and chopped*
⅓   *cup minced green onions or chives*

- Pour boiling water over Bulgur and let stand 10 minutes. Drain and set aside.
- In a large mixing bowl, stir together flour, cornmeal, Parmesan cheese, sugar, baking powder, oregano and pepper. Set aside.
- In another bowl, beat eggs slightly. Add milk, oil, drained Bulgur and Cheddar cheese; stir and add to dry mixture stirring just to moisten. Fold in tomatoes and onion.
- Grease a 9x5x3-inch loaf pan and sprinkle sides and bottom with cornmeal.
- Pour batter into prepared pan and bake at 375 degrees for 40 minutes. Cover loosely with foil and continue baking 10 to 15 minutes longer or until top is golden. Cool pan on rack. Serve warm or cold.

ONION CORNBREAD

Serves 8 to 10

2 to 3 large sweet onions
½ cup butter
1 14-ounce package corn muffin mix
2 eggs, beaten
⅔ cup milk
1 17-ounce can cream corn
4 drops red pepper sauce
2 cups sour cream
½ teaspoon salt
½ teaspoon dill weed
2 cups grated Cheddar cheese divided

- Peel and chop onions. Sauté slowly in butter; set aside.
- Combine corn muffin mix, eggs, milk, corn and red pepper sauce. Pour into a greased 9x13-inch baking dish.
- Add sour cream, salt, dill and 1 cup cheese to onions. Spread on mix. Sprinkle second cup of cheese over all.
- Bake at 400 degrees for 20 to 23 minutes. Cut into squares. Serve warm.

This will freeze well!

RHUBARB COFFEE CAKE

Serves 8 to 10

½ cup shortening
2 cups sugar, divided
1 egg
1 cup buttermilk
2 cups flour
   pinch of salt
1 teaspoon baking soda
1 teaspoon vanilla
2 cups finely chopped rhubarb
1 teaspoon cinnamon

- In large mixing bowl, cream shortening and 1½ cups of sugar. Add egg and beat until smooth; add buttermilk and beat until well mixed.
- Gradually add the flour, salt and soda, then the vanilla. Fold in the rhubarb. Pour batter into a greased 9x13-inch baking dish.
- Mix ½ cup sugar with cinnamon and sprinkle over the top. Bake at 350 degrees for 35 to 45 minutes.

SPICED PRUNE AND ALMOND COFFEE CAKE

Serves 10 to 12

¾ cup whole, unblanched almonds, toasted and
   finely chopped
1 cup buttermilk
2½ tablespoons instant coffee granules
1 teaspoon vanilla
½ teaspoon almond extract
2½ cups flour
2 teaspoons baking powder
1 teaspoon baking soda
1 teaspoon cinnamon
1 teaspoon salt
¼ teaspoon ground cloves
1 cup butter or margarine at room temperature
1 cup sugar
3 large eggs
1 cup finely chopped prunes, or other dried fruit
1 tablespoon grated orange rind

Glaze

½ cup firmly packed brown sugar
¼ cup butter or margarine
¼ cup whipping cream
1 teaspoon instant coffee granules

- Sprinkle half of the almonds into a buttered 10-inch bundt pan.
- Combine buttermilk, coffee granules, vanilla and almond extract in small bowl and stir until coffee dissolves.
- Sift flour, baking powder, soda, cinnamon, salt and cloves into medium bowl.
- Cream butter and sugar in large bowl; add eggs one at a time.
- Slowly add dry ingredients alternately with buttermilk mixture. Mix in prunes and orange rind.
- Pour batter into pan. Sprinkle with remaining almonds and bake at 350 degrees for 50 minutes or until wooden pick comes out clean. Cool 30 minutes and turn out onto rack.

Glaze

- Combine brown sugar, butter or margarine and cream in small pan; bring to a boil, stirring constantly. Boil 2 minutes; mix in coffee granules. Cool slightly and drizzle over cake.

FRESH APPLE COFFEE CAKE

Serves 6

2 cups chopped apple
½ cup chopped nuts
1 cup flour
½ teaspoon salt
1 teaspoon soda
1 egg
¼ cup salad oil
1 cup sugar
1 teaspoon ground cinnamon
¼ teaspoon ground nutmeg

- Process nuts and apples together briefly in food processor, or chop by hand. Add all other ingredients in order given. Blend briefly until flour is moist.
- Spread in a greased 8-inch square baking pan.
- Bake at 350 degrees for 40 to 45 minutes, or until a wooden pick comes out clean. Let stand in pan for 10 minutes before turning out on wire rack.

May be made in muffin cups as well. Very moist and flavorful!

KRISTIANA KRINGLER

Serves 8 to 12

2 cups flour, divided
1 cup plus 1 teaspoon butter, divided
1 cup plus 2 tablespoons water, divided
3 eggs
¼ teaspoon salt
1 teaspoon almond flavoring, divided
1 cup powdered sugar

- Mix 1 cup flour, ½ cup butter and 2 tablespoons water as for a pie crust. Divide dough in half and place in 2 strips, 3 inches wide, the length of an ungreased cookie sheet.
- In a saucepan, bring 1 cup water and ½ cup butter to a boil. Remove from heat; add 1 cup flour and stir until smooth.
- Add eggs, one at a time, beating until smooth. Add the salt and ½ teaspoon almond flavoring. Spread on top of unbaked strips of dough.
- Bake at 375 degrees for 45 minutes.
- When cool, frost with a mixture of 1 teaspoon butter, 1 cup powdered sugar and ½ teaspoon almond flavoring.

SWEET
ENDINGS

ALMOND BLOSSOM CAKE

Serves 10 to 12

2 cups all-purpose flour
1 teaspoon baking soda
1 teaspoon baking powder
¼ teaspoon salt
1 cup sugar
½ cup plus 1 tablespoon butter
2 eggs, beaten
1 teaspoon vanilla
1 cup yogurt
1½ cups sliced almonds, toasted, divided
½ cup half and half
¼ cup brandy
1 8-ounce can blanched almond paste
4 tablespoons milk
4 tablespoons powdered sugar
  sliced toasted almonds for garnish

- Sift first 4 ingredients; set aside.
- Cream sugar and ½ cup butter. Add beaten eggs and vanilla; blend well. Add dry ingredients to butter mixture alternately with yogurt; batter will be stiff. Stir in 1 cup almonds; set aside.
- Combine half and half, brandy and remaining ½ cup almonds; set aside.
- Knead almond paste with fingers until soft and pliable; add to brandy mixture a little at a time until well blended; mixture will be slightly lumpy.
- Spread ½ of the cake batter in greased and floured 9 or 10-inch tube pan. Spread ½ of almond paste mixture over cake batter. Spread remaining batter over almond paste mixture.
- To remaining almond paste mixture add milk and powdered sugar. Pour over cake. Bake at 350 degrees for 30 minutes.
- Remove from oven and garnish top with sliced almonds. Bake 30 minutes longer or until toothpick inserted in center comes out clean. Cool on wire rack 30 minutes. Carefully remove from pan and cool completely. Heat remaining tablespoon butter and brush top of cake.

Decorate cake plates with fresh blossoms for a "pretty as a picture" presentation.

CREAMY CHOCOLATE ROLL

Serves 12

¾ cup all-purpose flour
¼ cup unsweetened powdered cocoa
1 teaspoon baking powder
¼ teaspoon salt
1 egg
1 cup granulated sugar
⅓ cup water
1 teaspoon vanilla
3 egg whites
5 tablespoons powdered sugar, divided

Ricotta Filling

2 cups part-skim ricotta cheese
3 tablespoons powdered sugar
¼ cup finely chopped candied orange peel
½ teaspoon almond extract

- Lightly grease a rimmed 10x15-inch baking dish and line it with wax paper; grease paper. In a bowl, mix flour, cocoa, baking powder and salt.
- In large bowl of an electric mixer, beat egg at high speed until thick and lemon-colored. Gradually add granulated sugar; continue to beat, scraping bowl often, until mixture is creamy and pale. Beat in water and vanilla. Fold in flour mixture.
- In small bowl of mixer, using clean, dry beaters, beat egg whites until they hold stiff peaks. Fold into batter. Pour into prepared pan; spread evenly.
- Bake in a 375 degree oven until top of cake springs back when lightly pressed, about 10 minutes. Immediately invert cake onto a dishtowel sprinkled with 3 tablespoons of the powdered sugar. Peel off wax paper; immediately roll cake and towel into a cylinder, starting with a short side. Let cool completely on a rack.
- Combine all ingredients for ricotta filling in small bowl of an electric mixer. Beat until well blended.
- Unroll cooled cake, spread with filling, and reroll. Do not be concerned if cake cracks. Wrap filled cake in plastic wrap and refrigerate for at least 2 hours or up to 24 hours. Sift remaining powdered sugar over cake before serving.

Make a chocoholic happy without all the calories.

CARROT CAKE

Serves 12 to 24

1   cup all-purpose flour
1   cup whole wheat flour
1½ tablespoons ground cinnamon
1   teaspoon ground nutmeg
2   teaspoons baking soda
2   teaspoons baking powder
½   teaspoon salt
1   cup firmly packed brown sugar
½   cup granulated sugar
1   8-ounce can crushed pineapple packed in its own juice
¾   cup salad oil
6   egg whites
1   teaspoon vanilla
3   cups finely shredded carrots
1½ cups golden raisins
1½ cups sifted powdered sugar

- In a large bowl, stir together all-purpose flour, whole wheat flour, cinnamon, nutmeg, baking soda, baking powder, salt, brown sugar and granulated sugar. Set aside.
- Drain pineapple, reserving juice for glaze. Place pineapple, oil, egg whites, vanilla and carrots in large bowl of an electric mixer and beat well until combined. Add pineapple mixture and raisins to flour mixture; stir until evenly moistened. Spoon into a well-greased, flour-dusted 9x13-inch baking dish.
- Bake in a 350 degree oven until a wooden pick inserted in center of cake comes out clean, about 45 minutes. Let cool in pan on a rack.
- Mix 1½ cups sifted powdered sugar and about ¼ cup of the reserved pineapple juice until mixture is smoothly blended and has a good pouring consistency; pour over cake. To serve, cut into about 2-inch squares.

A much lighter version of an old time favorite.

WENATCHEE APPLE CAKE

Serves 12 to 15

1½ cups grated raw apples, unpeeled
 3 tablespoons water
 2 teaspoons soda, divided
 ½ cup shortening
 1 cup sugar
 2 cups flour
1½ tablespoons cocoa
 1 teaspoon nutmeg
 1 teaspoon allspice
 1 teaspoon cinnamon
 ½ teaspoon salt
 1 teaspoon vanilla
 1 cup raisins or dates
 1 cup nuts
 2 tablespoons orange juice
 2 tablespoons sugar
    butter

- Mix apples with water and 1 teaspoon soda. Let stand.
- Cream shortening and 1 cup sugar.
- Sift dry ingredients together.
- Combine shortening mixture, apples and dry ingredients. Stir in vanilla, raisins or dates and nuts. Bake in greased 9x5-inch loaf pan at 350 degrees for 1 hour.
- Combine orange juice with 2 tablespoons sugar for an orange topping. While cake is hot, dot top with butter and pour topping on cake for glaze.

BREAD PUDDING WITH SHERRY SAUCE

Serves 12

3½   cups skim milk

¾   cup sugar

3   eggs or 1 egg plus 4 egg whites

½   cup raisins

2   tablespoons vanilla extract

1   teaspoon ground cinnamon

9   1-ounce slices French bread, cut into ¾-inch cubes

2   tablespoons butter or margarine, melted
vegetable cooking spray
Sherry Sauce

- Combine milk and next 6 ingredients in a large bowl; toss gently. Let mixture stand one hour.
- Add butter or margarine; toss gently. Spoon mixture into a 9x13-inch baking dish coated with cooking spray. Bake at 350 degrees for 45 minutes or until pudding is set. Serve warm or at room temperature with Sherry Sauce.

A low fat version of an old favorite.

SHERRY SAUCE

Makes About 1 Cup

½   cup butter

1   cup sugar

½   cup evaporated milk or cream
pinch of salt

3 to 4   tablespoons cream sherry

¾   teaspoon vanilla extract

- Mix the butter, sugar, milk or cream and salt in a saucepan. Place over medium heat and stir constantly until butter is melted. Cook about 4 to 5 minutes more, continually stirring. Watch carefully that mixture does not burn.
- Remove from heat and cool slightly, then add sherry and vanilla.

Use the very best ingredients and you will find the taste wonderful. Serve over ice cream, apple or mincemeat pie, bread pudding, etc. Great for the holidays!

ORANGE-APPLE STRUDEL

Serves 10

2   *pounds tart green-skinned apples, such as Granny Smith*

2   *teaspoons grated orange peel*

½   *cup firmly packed brown sugar*

¼   *cup all-purpose flour*

1   *teaspoon ground cinnamon*

½   *teaspoon ground nutmeg*

3   *sheets filo pastry, thawed if frozen*

2   *tablespoons margarine, melted, divided Orange Sauce*

Orange Sauce

1   *tablespoon cornstarch*

1   *tablespoon water*

1   *cup orange juice*

¼   *cup orange marmalade*

- Peel and core apples, then thinly slice them into a large bowl. Mix in orange peel, sugar, flour, cinnamon and nutmeg.

- Lay one sheet of pastry on a baking sheet. With a pastry brush, lightly brush pastry with 1½ teaspoons of the margarine. Stack remaining 2 filo sheets on top, brushing each with 1½ teaspoons margarine. Then spoon apple mixture in a strip down one long side of stacked filo sheets, 1½ inches in from side and extending to about 1 inch from ends. Fold ends of filo over filling, then roll up filo jelly-roll style, starting at side nearest filling. Brush with remaining 1½ teaspoons margarine.

- Bake in a 375 degree oven until pastry is rich golden brown, about 45 minutes. Meanwhile, prepare Orange Sauce. Let strudel cool on baking sheet on a rack. Serve warm or at room temperature.

- To serve, cut crosswise; pour 2 tablespoons Orange Sauce over slices.

Orange Sauce

- In a 1 to 2-quart pan, stir together cornstarch and water. Add orange juice and orange marmalade. Bring to a boil over high heat, stirring.

- Serve hot or at room temperature. If made ahead, cover and refrigerate until next day; before serving, bring to room temperature or stir over medium-high heat until hot, about 2 minutes.

Filo dough lightens up this old time favorite.

PUMPKIN CHIFFON PIE

Serves 6 to 8

1 envelope unflavored gelatin
⅔ cup brown sugar, packed
½ teaspoon salt
½ teaspoon cinnamon
½ teaspoon nutmeg
½ teaspoon ginger
1¼ cups canned pumpkin
3 egg yolks
½ cup milk
3 egg whites
½ cup sugar
1 9-inch baked pie shell
  whipped cream or frozen whipped topping

- Blend gelatin, brown sugar, seasonings, pumpkin, egg yolks and milk in a saucepan. Cook over medium heat, stirring constantly. Cook just to a boil. Remove from heat. Set pan in ice water and stir mixture until it mounds when dropped from a spoon.
- Beat egg whites until stiff peaks form. Gradually blend in sugar. Gently fold this meringue into the cooled pumpkin mixture. Pour into baked pie shell and chill at least 2 hours. Serve with whipped cream or frozen whipped topping.

A traditional holiday meal ending!

FRESH FRUIT TART

Serves 6 to 8

¼ cup powdered sugar
1 cup flour
½ cup butter
  fruit to cover 10-inch round pan with removable bottom (strawberries, raspberries or a mixture of fruits)

Glaze

2 tablespoons cornstarch
2 tablespoons sugar
⅔ cup orange juice
½ cup red currant jelly

- Sift powdered sugar and flour together. Rub butter into flour and sugar mixture. Press into a 10-inch round pan with removable bottom; prick all over with fork.
- Bake at 350 degrees for 15 to 20 minutes. Cool. Cover base with fruit.
- Combine ingredients for glaze and cook for 2 minutes. Pour over the fruit.

CINNAMON RHUBARB PINWHEELS

Serves 10 to 12

Sauce

       2   cups brown sugar
       2   cups water
     ¼   cup butter
     ½   teaspoon cinnamon

Pinwheels

       2   cups flour
     2½   teaspoons baking powder
     ½   teaspoon salt
     ⅔   cup plus 2 tablespoons butter
     ½   cup milk
       5   cups finely cut rhubarb
     ½   cup, or less, sugar
     ½   teaspoon cinnamon

Sauce

- Combine the brown sugar, water, butter and cinnamon in a pan. Bring to a boil and cook, uncovered, at a rolling boil for 5 minutes. Set aside while preparing pinwheels.

Pinwheels

- Sift flour, baking powder and salt. Cut in ⅔ cup butter. (Reserve 2 tablespoons.) Add the milk and mix to a soft dough. Roll out on a floured board to form a rectangle approximately 14 x 17-inches. Spread with reserved butter. Cover evenly with rhubarb and sprinkle with sugar mixed with cinnamon. Roll as for a jelly roll starting with the long side. Cut into 1-inch slices. Place cut side down in a greased 9x13-inch baking dish. Pour the prepared sauce over the slices.
- Bake at 375 degrees for 40 minutes. Serve hot or cold, with cream if desired.

A 16-ounce package of Scone and Shortcake Mix with ⅔ cup of milk may be used in place of the first five ingredients in the pinwheels.

WALNUT TORTE

Serves 6

2   *tablespoons unsalted butter*

1¼   *cups graham cracker crumbs, divided*

4   *egg whites*

¼   *teaspoon salt*

1   *cup sugar*

½   *cup chopped nut meats, use all black walnuts or*
     ¼ cup each black and English walnuts

½   *cup moist shredded coconut meat*

½   *teaspoon vanilla*

½   *pint whipping cream or ice cream (optional)*
     freshly grated nutmeg

- Butter a 12-inch round spring-form pan and dust with ¼ cup graham cracker crumbs.
- In large mixer bowl, whip egg whites and salt until stiff but not dry. Add sugar ¼ cup at a time. Add remaining crumbs, nuts, coconut and vanilla.
- Pour batter into pan and spread quickly and gently. Bake at 350 degrees for 25 to 30 minutes. Do not overbake. Test to be sure the center is not too soft. Cool in pan in oven with door ajar, but with no drafts.
- To serve, remove sides of pan and cut torte with a very sharp knife. Pass unsweetened whipped cream dusted lightly with freshly grated nutmeg, or ice cream.

ALMOND TARTS

Serves 6

Crust

6   *tablespoons butter*

¼   *cup sugar*

1   *cup flour*

Filling

2   *tablespoons butter*

¼   *cup sugar*

1½   *tablespoons cream*

2   *teaspoons flour*

⅓   *cup sliced almonds*

- Cream butter and sugar together for crust. Blend in flour until crumbly. Divide among six 4-inch tart pans or use smaller pans for more tarts. Press into bottom and slightly up the sides. Bake at 350 degrees for 10 minutes or until lightly browned.
- In a small saucepan, on low heat, cook the filling ingredients until the sugar is dissolved. Divide the filling among the tart pans. Return to the oven for 10 to 15 minutes or until filling is bubbly. Watch carefully as the tarts burn readily. Cool before popping out of tart pans.

These tarts freeze well. An original recipe from Sweden around the turn of the century.

BAKED QUINCE

Serves 6

6   *small quince*
¾   *cup sugar, divided*
      salt (optional)
1⅓ *cups hot water*

❧ Peel, core and slice the quince. Arrange quince, ½ cup sugar, salt, and water in a casserole dish, layering the quince and sprinkling the sugar on each layer. Cover and bake at 325 degrees for 2 hours or until tender and the color is a deep red.

❧ Remove the cover, sprinkle with ¼ cup sugar and continue baking, uncovered, until the syrup is somewhat thickened. Serve either hot or cold. Ice cream on the cold version enhances the serving.

Beautiful red color and so tasty.

NO-HASSLE DESSERT PIZZA

Serves 12

    non-stick cooking spray
1   *20-ounce package chocolate-chip cookie dough*
1   *package vanilla-flavored instant pudding*
1¼ *cups milk*
¼   *teaspoon almond extract*
1   *medium sized banana, sliced*
½   *pint blackberries*
4   *kiwifruit, peeled and sliced*
5   *large plums, thinly sliced*

❧ Spray a 14-inch pizza pan with cooking spray. With floured hands, press cookie dough to cover bottom of pan. Bake at 350 degrees for 12 to 15 minutes. Cool crust on wire rack.

❧ Prepare pudding per directions, but use 1¼ cups milk and add almond extract.

❧ Spread filling on cool cookie crust. Arrange fruit on pudding. Refrigerate before serving.

WINE BASTED PEARS

Serves 6

6 *pears, slightly under-ripe*
2 *tablespoons lemon juice*
2 *cups hearty red wine such as Zinfandel or*
   Burgundy
1 *teaspoon honey*
2 *teaspoons cinnamon*
1 *cup orange juice*
   fresh mint leaves for garnish

- Core whole pears from bottom, leaving stems intact. Peel pears.
- In a deep saucepan mix remaining ingredients except mint leaves and bring to a boil. Add pears and simmer until they become deep red in color and softened, about 35 minutes.
- Drain pears and chill, reserving liquid for another use. Garnish with mint leaves and serve.

The alcohol in the wine evaporates, along with about 80% of the wine's original calories. Only the aroma and flavor remain!

BLUEBERRY BUTTERMILK SHERBET

Serves 6

2 *cups fresh or unsweetened frozen blueberries*
2 *teaspoons grated lemon peel*
2 *tablespoons lemon juice*
¼ *cup sugar*
1 *cup buttermilk*

- Rinse and drain blueberries; put in a 2 to 3-quart pan. Add lemon peel, lemon juice and sugar. Cook over medium-high heat, stirring often, until mixture is simmering and blueberries begin to pop, about 6 minutes.
- Chill until cool or up to 24 hours.
- In a blender or food processor, purée the mixture with buttermilk until smooth.
- Pour into a 9 to 10-inch square metal pan. Cover and freeze until solid, at least 4 hours.
- Break mixture into chunks; whirl in a food processor or beat with a mixer until smooth. Return to pan.
- Cover and freeze until ready to use, at least 30 minutes or up to one week. Let hard-frozen sherbet soften slightly before serving.

RASPBERRY SORBET

Serves 4

1½ *teaspoons unflavored gelatin*
½ *cup water*
1 *10-ounce package frozen raspberries with syrup, partially thawed*
⅓ *cup raspberry-flavored liqueur*
2 *tablespoons lemon juice*

- In small sauce pan, combine gelatin and water; let stand one minute. Stir over medium heat until gelatin dissolves; set aside.
- In food processor bowl with metal blade or blender container, place partially thawed fruit; process until smooth. Add liqueur, lemon juice and gelatin mixture; process until smooth.
- Pour sorbet into 9-inch square pan; cover. Freeze until almost firm, 3 to 5 hours, stirring occasionally.
- Spoon partially frozen sorbet mixture into food processor bowl with metal blade or large bowl; process or beat at medium speed until mixture is smooth and fluffy, but not thawed.
- Transfer to covered container; freeze until firm, at least 4 to 6 hours. Serve with papaya, kiwifruit and fresh raspberries, if desired.

Fast, easy, colorful!

CHOCOLATE-DIPPED OATMEAL LACE COOKIES
Makes 30 Cookies

1   large egg, beaten lightly
¼   cup firmly packed light brown sugar
¼   cup granulated sugar
1   cup old-fashioned rolled oats
¼   teaspoon salt
¼   teaspoon almond extract
1   tablespoon unsalted butter, melted and cooled
4   ounces semi-sweet chocolate, coarsely chopped

- Beat egg with sugars until mixture is thick and pale; add oats, salt, almond extract and butter and combine well.
- Line baking sheets with buttered foil. Drop batter by rounded teaspoonful 3 inches apart onto baking sheets. Flatten each mound with the back of a fork dipped in water.
- Bake at 325 degrees for 7 minutes or until golden around the edges. Let cool on baking sheets and gently peel away from the foil.
- Melt chocolate in top of double boiler set over barely simmering water.
- Holding each cookie by the edge, dip into chocolate to coat half. Put cookies on racks while the chocolate hardens.

CHOCOLATE MEXICAN COOKIES
Makes 4 Dozen

1½   cups sifted flour
¾   cup unsweetened cocoa powder
¼   teaspoon salt
     generous pinch of ground black pepper
     generous pinch of cayenne pepper
¾   teaspoon cinnamon
¾   cup unsalted butter
1½   teaspoons vanilla
1   cup sugar
1   egg

- Sift together flour, cocoa, salt, pepper, cayenne and cinnamon.
- Cream the butter, vanilla and sugar. Add egg and mix.
- Gradually add sifted dry ingredients, scraping bowl and beating only until mixed.
- On waxed paper, shape the dough into a cylinder about ten inches long, two inches in diameter. Freeze or refrigerate.
- At baking time, cut into slices ¼ inch thick. Bake at 375 degrees for 10 to 12 minutes. Watch carefully so cookies do not burn.

CHOCOLATE CHOCOLATE COOKIES

Makes 5 to 6 Dozen

  4 *ounces unsweetened chocolate*
  3 *cups semi-sweet chocolate chips, divided*
  ½ *cup unsalted butter*
  ½ *cup flour*
  ½ *teaspoon double-acting baking powder*
  ½ *teaspoon salt*
  4 *large eggs*
 1½ *cups sugar*
  2 *teaspoons vanilla*
 1½ *tablespoons instant espresso powder (optional)*

- In top of double boiler, melt unsweetened chocolate, 1½ cups chocolate chips and butter.
- In small bowl, stir together the flour, baking powder and salt.
- In large bowl, beat eggs and sugar until mixture is thick and pale. Beat in vanilla and espresso powder.
- Fold the chocolate mixture into the egg mixture, then fold in flour mixture and remaining chocolate chips. Let stand for 15 minutes.
- Drop by spoonful on parchment paper or aluminum foil. Bake at 350 degrees for 12 to 15 minutes or until cracked and shiny on top. Do not overbake. Allow to cool completely before removing them from paper or foil.

Possibly the most sinful cookies you will ever eat!

LEMON RHUBARB GLORIES

Make 24 Squares

Crust

   1   *cup flour*
   ¼   *cup sugar*
   ½   *cup butter*

Filling

   1   *cup sugar*
   3   *tablespoons flour*
   2   *eggs, beaten*
   3   *tablespoons lemon juice*
   ½   *cup shredded unsweetened coconut*
   1   *cup finely diced rhubarb*
   1   *teaspoon vanilla*
       powdered sugar

- Mix together ingredients for crust and put into a greased 8x11-inch baking dish. Bake at 325 degrees for 15 minutes.
- Mix the filling ingredients, except powdered sugar, and pour over crust while still warm. Return to oven for 30 minutes. Sprinkle with powdered sugar and cool in the pan. Cut into squares while still warm.

Other fruit can be used, such as raspberries, strawberries and blueberries.

DATE NUT COOKIES

Makes 3 Dozen

   1   *cup butter or margarine*
   1   *cup brown sugar, firmly packed*
   ½   *cup sugar*
   2   *egg whites*
   2   *teaspoons vanilla*
   2   *cups flour*
   1   *teaspoon baking powder*
   ½   *teaspoon salt*
   1   *cup chopped dates*
   1   *cup chopped pecans or walnuts*

- Beat butter or margarine until light and fluffy. Gradually beat in sugars. Mix in egg whites and vanilla.
- Mix flour with baking powder and salt. Combine flour and butter mixtures and beat until well blended. Stir in dates and nuts.
- Drop by rounded teaspoonful onto ungreased baking sheets, placing cookies about 2 inches apart. Bake at 375 degrees for 8 minutes or until lightly browned.

This dough is a basic chocolate chip recipe, but you'll be surprised how differently they taste. Very rich and chewy!

PUMPKIN DATE COOKIES

Makes 2 to 3 Dozen

¼   *cup shortening*
½   *cup sugar*
1   *egg*
½   *cup canned pumpkin*
1   *cup sifted flour*
2   *teaspoons baking powder*
½   *teaspoon salt*
1¼   *teaspoons cinnamon*
⅛   *teaspoon ginger*
¼   *teaspoon nutmeg*
½   *cup chopped dates*
½   *cup chopped nuts*

Vanilla Butter Icing

3   *cups powdered sugar*
⅓   *cup butter, softened*
1½   *teaspoons vanilla*
2   *tablespoons milk*

❧ Cream shortening and sugar. Add egg and beat well. Blend in pumpkin.

❧ Sift flour, measure and add other dry ingredients. Stir into the creamed mixture with the dates and nuts that have been dredged in some of the flour.

❧ Drop by teaspoonful on greased baking sheets. Bake at 400 degrees for 8 to 10 minutes. Cool.

❧ Prepare vanilla butter icing by mixing powdered sugar and butter; stir in vanilla and milk. Beat until smooth and spreadable. Frost cooled cookies.

Nice for Halloween or Thanksgiving!

DUTCH ALMOND COOKIES

Makes About 8 Dozen

2¾ cups flour

2 teaspoons cinnamon

½ teaspoon nutmeg

¼ teaspoon baking soda

1 cup soft butter or margarine

1 cup light brown sugar

¼ cup plain yogurt

½ cup finely chopped, blanched almonds

- Sift together flour, cinnamon, nutmeg and baking soda. Set aside.
- In large bowl of mixer, beat butter or margarine, sugar and yogurt until smooth and fluffy. At low speed, beat in half the flour mixture. Beat in the other half and the almonds to form a stiff dough.
- Divide dough in half and form each half into a roll about seven inches long.
- Wrap each roll in wax paper and refrigerate eight hours or freeze for later use.
- Slice each roll into ⅛ to ¼-inch slices and bake at 375 degrees for 8 to 10 minutes.

Happy is the gardener who has a few rolls of refrigerator cookies in the freezer so that on a sunny day she can be out in the garden and still have fresh cookies!

SIMPLE SESAMES

Makes 4 Dozen

2 cups butter, softened
1½ cups sugar
3 cups all-purpose flour
1 cup sesame seeds
2 cups shredded coconut
½ cup finely chopped almonds

❧ In a large mixer bowl cream butter. Gradually add sugar and continue beating until light and fluffy. Add flour and mix just until combined. Stir in sesame seeds, coconut and almonds just until well mixed.

❧ Divide dough into thirds. Place one third on a long sheet of wax paper. Shape into a long roll 2 inches in diameter. Repeat with remaining dough. Wrap and refrigerate until firm.

❧ Cut rolls into ¼-inch slices. Bake on ungreased cookie sheets at 300 degrees for 30 minutes. Remove to wire racks to cool.

ROSEMARY THYME SHORTBREAD COOKIES

Makes 2 to 3 Dozen Small Cookies

¼ cup powdered sugar
9 tablespoons unsalted butter
½ teaspoon grated lemon rind
1½ cups flour
1½ tablespoons fresh rosemary, finely chopped
2 teaspoons fresh thyme, finely chopped
1 tablespoon granulated sugar

- Work together the sugar, butter and lemon rind; add flour, rosemary and thyme. Knead together to make a soft dough.
- Carefully roll out the dough to about 3⁄8-inch thick. Cut into squares, rounds or other small shapes—leaves are nice.
- Bake on a greased cookie sheet at 350 degrees for 15 to 20 minutes or until the cookies are a light golden color. Do not overbake.
- Sprinkle cookies with granulated sugar. Cool and store in an airtight container.

Lemon thyme is nice to use if you have it.

SEVEN LAYER COOKIES

Makes 2 Dozen

½ cup butter or margarine, melted
1 cup graham cracker crumbs
1 7-ounce package peanut butter chips
1 7-ounce package chocolate chips
1 cup flaked coconut
1 can sweetened condensed milk
1 cup chopped nuts

- Put melted butter or margarine in 9x13-inch pan. Add, in layers, graham cracker crumbs, peanut butter chips, chocolate chips and coconut.
- Drizzle milk over all. Add nuts last and pat into place.
- Bake at 350 degrees for 20 to 25 minutes.

CONTRIBUTORS

CONTRIBUTORS

The Cookbook Committee and The Arboretum Foundation express grateful appreciation to Foundation members and friends who contributed recipes to "The Cultivated Palate." We also thank the testers, proofreaders and other volunteers who have helped immeasurably throughout the entire cookbook production process. Unfortunately we were unable to include all the many recipes which were submitted, due to similarity or availability of space.

Martha Aigner
June Alvord
Aileen Anderson
Jan McPhee Anderson
Deborah Andrews
Jim Andrews M.D.
Susan C. Ayrault
Nan Ballard
Jeannine Bannick
Vera Baumgartner
Pat Boehm
Norma Brady
Betty Brokaw
Gail Bronson
Cecelia Buck
Helen Bucy
Adele Burnett
Elizabeth A. Carter
Georgiana Chave
Mary A. Chrismer
Jo Ann Clark
Lee Clarke
Elaine Cochran
Roseanne Cohn
Dorothy Colby
Ruth Collins
Sabra Contreras
Vonnie Cowan
Leo Cunningham
Vernette Cunningham
Jeannine Curry

Sarma Davidson
Ruth Day
Sally Day
Barbara Donley
Maggie Dorsey
Barby Doss
Marge Dudley
Wendy Eacret
Patti J. Eckoff
June Emmons
Nuki Fellows
Hazel Fiedler
Susan Foe
Barbara Friend
Jeanne Gardiner
Lynn Garvey
Betty Gray
Greta Hackett
Karen Hamilton
Clem Hamilton, Phd
Barbara Harris
Esther Hazelet
Donna Henry
Elizabeth Herman
Joy Herring
Joanne Hochberg
Joan H. Hoeft
Gerry Holley
Luanna Iverson
Effie Jacobson
Caroline Johnson

Becky Johnson
Velma Johnston
Violet Johnston
Peter Kahn
Barbara Keightley
Hazel Kelly
Karole Kiefer
Joan King
Virginia P. Kitchell
Janet Klos
Elizabeth A. Kruse
Tina Kuhnle
Frances Kwapil
Rita Lambro
Cara Larsen
Denise Larsen
Doris Lawler
Irene LeClair
Beverly Leitch
Harriet Litt
Jody Logan
Ann Lovejoy
Elaine Lovelace
Mavis Mackay
Susie Marglin
Anne Martin
Rozanne Mascio
Kay Mayhew
Betty McGraw
Harriet McLean
Judy McPhedran

Marilyn Mechelsen
Jean Mills
Lucy Mitchell
Virginia Morell
Elizabeth Moses
Susan G. Moss
Mary Ellen Mulder
Margaret Mulligan
Betty Murvin
Nancy Nashy
Jane Nelson
Marilou Nichols
Helen O'Burube
Penny O'Byrne
Ann O'Mera
Kay Ogle
The Patricia Calvert
  Greenhouse Cookbook
Janet Patrick
Sharon Patrick
Carole Pearl
Ruth Perkins
Sally Peterson
Mary Pinkam
Jan Pirzio-Biroli
Jo Pistole
Terry Pottmeyer

Pat Pruss
Ginny Puckett
Lynda Ransley
Mary Lou Richardson
Carol Robbins
Frances Ross
Ellen Rossen
Gerry Ruhland
Barbara Rumpf
Dori Schiller
Mary Ann Schnaidt
Richard Schultz
Janice Scott
Susan Shea
Sue Sherwood
James Shigeta
Carol Simons
Christa Sinton
June Skidmore
Charity Small
Mary Smith
Ken Sorrells
Arlene Sourbeer
Joy Spurr
Mary K. Sutter
Barbara Tapa
Dianne Taylor

Robert H. Thompson
Mary Thorne
Mary Ann Trombold
Karen Trout
Contributors to Unit 24's
  "A Gardner's Kitchen"
Members of Unit 26
Members of Unit 53
Ruth Vorobik
Winette Waggoner
Margaret Waldo
Sandy Walker
Steve Walker
Siri Watt
Fred and Ann Weinmann
The West Seattle Garden Club
Joanne White
Ellen Widmayer
Ellen L. Willner
Alice Wilson
Jean Witt
Molly Wolfe
Betty Wood
John A. Wott, Phd
Annette Wright
Sandy Yeager
Charlotte Zila-Turner

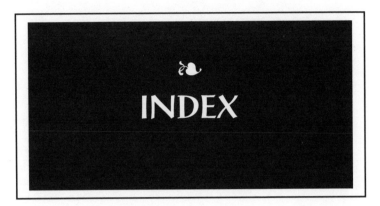

INDEX